Encouraging Learning

Over the last 20 years James Nottingham has studied how children learn. He has taught every age group in both primary and secondary schools, helped deaf teenagers deal with anger and isolation and even done philosophy with three-year-olds.

In this inspiring, humorous and practical book he shows what *you* can do to help children of all ages develop into confident, thoughtful and independent learners. Based around the acronym ASK, this book explores attitudes, skills and knowledge to learning – what is required and how to develop these skills more effectively. It shows how to encourage independent thinking and a spirit of inquiry in your children.

Highlights include:

- the dangers of calling our children clever, bright and gifted;
- the best ways to teach wisdom;
- how to help children excel in exams; and
- why curiosity did *not* kill the cat.

With a foreword written by **John Hattie**, *Encouraging Learning* draws on research from some of the most respected experts on thinking and learning to identify the best ways to help children learn more effectively, efficiently and co-operatively.

For everyone living or working with children – particularly teachers, parents, carers and youth workers – this book shows you some of the best ways to enhance children's learning, including how to question, praise and encourage more effectively.

James Nottingham is an internationally known freelance trainer and educational consultant, as well as Director of JN Partnership Ltd. Formerly a teacher and leader in both primary and secondary schools in the UK, he is also co-founder of www.p4c.com, an international resource and collaboration cooperative for Philosophy for Children.

Encouraging Learning

How you can help children learn

James Nottingham

Routledge
Taylor & Francis Group

LONDON AND NEW YORK

This edition published 2013
by Routledge
2 Park Square, Milton Park, Abingdon, Oxon OX14 4RN

Simultaneously published in the USA and Canada
by Routledge
711 Third Avenue, New York, NY 10017

Routledge is an imprint of the Taylor & Francis Group, an informa business

First published in Australia by Hawker Brownlow in 2012

British Library Cataloguing in Publication Data
A catalogue record for this book is available from the British Library

Library of Congress Cataloging in Publication Data
A catalog record for this book has been requested

ISBN: 978-0-415-82172-8 (hbk)
ISBN: 978-0-415-82173-5 (pbk)
ISBN: 978-0-203-55907-9 (ebk)

Typeset in Bembo and Helvetica Neue
by Florence Production Ltd, Stoodleigh, Devon, UK

MIX
Paper from
responsible sources
FSC   FSC® C013056
www.fsc.org

Printed and bound in Great Britain by
TJ International Ltd, Padstow, Cornwall

This book is dedicated to:
Jill, Ava, Harry and Phoebe
My family, my world

We now accept the fact that learning is a lifelong process of keeping abreast of change. And the most pressing task is to teach people how to learn.

(Peter Drucker, 1909–2005, described by *Business Week* as 'the man who invented management')[1]

Contents

Foreword

The book begins with the ever-present question – What is the point of education? Nottingham answers simply, directly and powerfully – to help children learn how to learn. He then concentrates on three major parts of learning: attitudes, skills and knowledge. He gives many examples of different ways we can learn to learn and what we can do to enhance such learning. He argues for more clever effort; challenging tests; a growth mindset; and he introduces fascinating terms such as 'wobblers' and 'going into the pit'.

Indeed, Nottingham's case is so compelling that it creates an enigma – why isn't learning to learn ever present in education? Teachers would say it is because of the pressures of examinations, curricula and timetables. Curriculum documents make claims to be about learning to learn but then fill the pages with content – they tend to look backwards to what others claim we need to know and in what order. Yet, most curricula are created by 'group think', with adults making decisions that are rarely based on how students actually progress through challenging ideas. Too many times material is presented that is not challenging to many in the class so the focus becomes on completing some activity rather than engaging in learning to deal with challenges, uncertainty, learning strategies of learning and enjoying the thrill of meeting challenge. Without challenge it is unlikely that learning to learn is of much use. This is an argument that resonates throughout Nottingham's book.

If you read this book from the perspective of a teacher or parent then there are powerful ideas for learning strategies. If you read this book from the student perspective then the main messages are to learn to be your own teacher; to teach yourselves how to strategise; when to use various learning notions; and know how to evaluate the effectiveness of your chosen strategies. As Nottingham shows, it is a mind set or a way of thinking about what we do in learning that matters.

My mantra has been that teachers need to see learning through the eyes and minds of students, and students need to learn to become their own teachers. Nottingham has provided a most worthwhile set of practical ideas based on developing this mindset with all learners.

Professor John Allan Hattie, Director of Melbourne
Education Research Institute, 10 September 2012

1

Learning *how* to learn

What's the point of education?

What's the point of education? I've been asked this a few times by pupils, a lot of times by adults who hated school and by more taxi drivers than I care to remember. My answer is always the same: to help children learn *how* to learn.

Of course this isn't the only goal. Children also need to become numerate, literate, thoughtful and kind. They need to understand how to act morally, considerately and socially. And they should know how to be safe.

Yet the almost daily debate in media around the world is about what *knowledge* ought to be taught in school. Recent debates have included whether creationism should be taught alongside evolution theory or whether there's a point to teaching *PowerPoint* when it'll probably be outmoded within a few years. There have been suggestions that if Latin were still on the curriculum then we'd all be language experts and that if the army ran our schools there'd be less crime. I even read recently that some dog trainers are insisting all children be taught at school how to recognise whether a dog is about to bite or beg! As important a lesson as this might be, I wonder where it would fit into the school timetable. Perhaps between hieroglyphics and henna tattooing on a Friday afternoon, at the end of the 60-hour school week needed to accommodate the demands of every special interest group?

There is merit to the debates about which subjects children should study. After all, pupils have to study something so it is right and proper that we consider which subjects are the most important. Yet think of all the information you learned at school. How much of it do you use today? Indeed, how much of it has been superseded by changes in society? Is there any point teaching today's children to map read, speak French, type on a keyboard, maintain a petrol-driven car (or even to drive)? If so, are these worthy enough to keep Mandarin Chinese, computer programming, or even dog whispering off the 25-hour weekly school timetable?

As a parent, I would like my children to learn French at school because I think learning other languages opens doors socially, emotionally and cognitively. However, if they don't manage to – well, *c'est la vie*.

On the other hand, I'm not prepared to take such a relaxed view about learning *how* to learn. If my children leave school without a superb repertoire of learning capabilities, a willingness to inquire and innovate and the wisdom to make judicious decisions (*as well as* lots of knowledge), I would feel that I, and their schooling, had let them down.

Yet how many children do leave school discouraged and ill-equipped for the intellectual and emotional challenges of life? How many leave school with good grades achieved through memorising facts, who then go on to struggle at university or work where the emphasis is on independent thinking not regurgitation?

Before we all rush to drag our kids out of school, the good news is that learning strategies *can* be taught, attitudes *can* be encouraged, motivation *can* be strengthened and many schools are succeeding admirably in achieving these ambitions.

The key is to recognise the value and role that attitudes, skills and knowledge play in the learning process and then to ensure that children's education involves a development of all three.

Here is where to start: A.S.K.

A.S.K

A.S.K stands for attitudes, skills and knowledge, which are made up of these key ingredients:

- **Attitudes** – positive attitudes towards learning, including curiosity and persistence.
- **Skills** – abilities to carry out those actions necessary for gaining understanding and achieving excellent performance in any given context.
- **Knowledge** – familiarity with information, concepts, theories and practices in a given field.

FIGURE 1.1 Developing attitudes, skills and knowledge

As a teacher in both primary and secondary schools, I used to plan lessons, set personalised goals for each pupil, and review learning with the help of the A.S.K model. I'd draw this as a triangle (below) to show that each lesson would emphasise two of the three dimensions of learning.

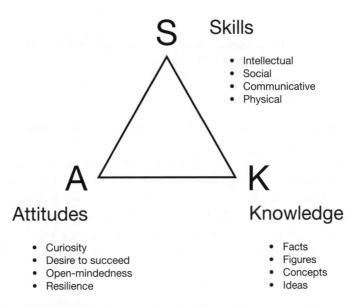

FIGURE 1.2 The A.S.K model triangle

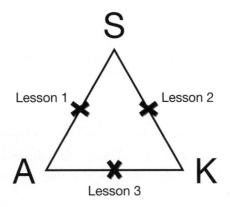

FIGURE 1.3 The A.S.K model triangle

For example, when we began a topic about the Vikings (a common theme in UK primary schools), the first three lessons would be along the lines of:

Lesson 1: Exercise our curiosity (attitude of curiosity) to create as many relevant questions (skill of asking relevant questions) about the Vikings.

Lesson 2: Decide which of our questions about Vikings has the most relevance to our topic (skill of prioritising by value) and which will help us to know most about lifestyles (knowledge about the Vikings).

Lesson 3: Gain knowledge of Vikings (knowledge about Viking history) by persisting (attitude of persistence) with answering the questions we struggled to answer last time.

Over the next few pages, I have listed the skills and attitudes displayed by the best learners I have encountered. You can discuss them with children in a number of ways.

For example:

(a) Talk about the attitudes that have helped you succeed and those that have led to problems.

(b) When watching a sporting event together (even if that's *Strictly*), draw attention to the competitors' desire to win, to take risks, and to focus on the outcome. You can also talk together about the attitudes the performers must have drawn upon to attain their high degree of proficiency.

(c) Identify the actions people can take to demonstrate particular attitudes – for example, having one more try when you feel like giving up would demonstrate determination.

(d) Talk about the progress your children have made in developing their skills – for example, how much they have improved in bike riding, writing, playing the guitar and so on.

Poor is the pupil who does not surpass his master

(Leonardo da Vinci, 1452–1519)

If we don't become better people from the education we gain, then what real purpose does education serve? If it is only to "earn" a living, then are we really "living"?

(Anon)

Attitudes for learning
S
K

Lev Vygotsky, one of the pioneers of educational psychology, wrote at length about cultural learning. He said children learn from those around them: what to laugh at, what to be afraid of, what to have a go at, what to avoid, and so on. He emphasised that children pick up mental, as well as physical, habits from their elders and warned us that the way we react to things is arguably more influential on young minds than the knowledge we share with children. In other words, children adopt many of our attitudes and values through dialogue with us. That's one heck of a responsibility for those of us with children in our lives!

Of course, there is no hierarchy or exhaustive list of attitudes, at least not that I'm aware of, but here are some that are displayed by the best learners I've come across.

Outstanding learners are:

- curious;
- focussed on what is relevant;
- full of wonder;
- keen to learn from mistakes;
- open to new experiences;
- persistent;
- resilient;
- risk takers;
- self-regulating;
- willing to ask for support and coaching.

> What (children) should learn first is not the subjects ordinarily taught, however important they may be; they should be given lessons of will, of attention, of discipline; before exercises in grammar, they need to be exercised in mental orthopaedics; in a word they must learn how to learn.
>
> (Alfred Binet, 1909, founder of IQ testing)[2]

An attitude of self-control

In 1972, Stanford University psychologist Walter Mischel conducted an experiment to find out when the trait of deferred gratification – the ability to wait for something you want – develops in children. The experiment has been repeated many times since, including in the BBC series *Child of Our Time*.

The original experiment involved more than 600 children between the ages of four and six. Sitting in an empty room, the children were offered a treat of their choice – a cookie, a pretzel or a marshmallow. They were each told they could eat their treat but if they could wait for 15 minutes without eating it then they would get a second one.

I encourage you to watch some of the video clips of similar experiments available online. In them you'll see some children refusing to look at their marshmallow, others peeking at it from behind their hands, one boy licking the plate but not the marshmallow and one even stroking it as if it were a pet!

In all, approximately one-third of the children were able to delay their gratification long enough to be rewarded with a second marshmallow. Of course, the older the child, the more likely they were to succeed but what Mischel also found from follow-up studies was:

> The children who could not wait were more likely to have behavioural problems both at home and school; they had lower exam scores; more often

FIGURE 1.4 Teaching self-control

struggled to deal with stressful situations or to pay attention; and found it more difficult to maintain friendships.

The children who were able to wait also craved the treat but were able to distract themselves by covering their eyes, playing hide and seek or singing songs. Their desire wasn't dispelled; it was merely forgotten.[3]

Forty years after the first experiment, the researchers tracked down sixty of the original participants and invited them to take part in a new study. They were shown a range of flash cards with faces displaying a range of expressions – happy, neutral or fearful – and asked to press a button every time they saw a fearful face.

This may seem an easy task but, as B. J. Casey, the neuropsychologist who carried out the tests along with Mischel, explains: 'A happy face is a social cue that is hard to resist' (ibid.). The results showed that the participants who had struggled to defer gratification when they were younger also struggled to resist pressing the button when they saw a happy face.

The experiment concluded with many of the participants repeating the test while lying in a brain scanner. The participants with better self-control showed more activity in the part of the brain associated with risk aversion, whereas those with poorer self-control showed increased activity in the brain region associated with reward and addiction.

The lesson of this study is that we should help children develop the capacity to wait or defer gratification. Telling them they shouldn't *want* something doesn't help; we can help them instead by teaching tactics to divert their attention, to focus on other things, to look forward, to plan and so on. Incidentally, this is partly why so many diets fail – we focus on the foods we shouldn't eat rather than on finding healthier foods or activities to distract us.

Teaching the attitude of self-control

Self-control develops with maturity and practice. Temperament also plays a role. Impetuous children may need more guidance, particularly in exciting or distracting situations; reflective children may appear more self-controlled when in fact they're just more reserved. Either way, explaining the reasons behind particular rules, teaching children how to focus and appealing to their sense of fairness should help develop their attitude. Modelling self-control always helps too!

For example:

(a) Saying no to the sweets they want but indulging in the treats you fancy will not help. Instead, draw attention to the things you'd like but are delaying acquiring and explain how you feel about this.

(b) Have a piggy bank or some visual means to demonstrate saving for things you want.

(c) Play games that reward self-control such as *Simon Says*, *Musical Statues* or *Wii Fitness*.

FIGURE 1.5 Cartoon of helicopter parents

Attitudes of parents

When I work in Australia, I often hear mention of 'helicopter parents' – the parents who 'hover' over their children, making sure they're safe, lending an overbearing hand, helping them to solve their quarrels, and so on.

In Scandinavia, they call them 'curling parents' – sweeping in front of their child, clearing the way just as, in the winter sport, a curler sweeps the ice in front of the curling stone.

Of course, I understand the need for our children to be safe – I've already got the shotgun and vicious dog on order to ward off suitors the day my daughter turns thirteen!

However, it baffles me how keen many of us are to erase problems from our children's lives: when our little darlings fall over, we rush to them, thus inferring that a tumble is something to wail about; when they get stuck on their homework, we do it for them; if they feel like giving up their hobby when the going gets tough, we seem quick to allow them to quit rather than using the opportunity to help them build a 'stick-to-it' attitude.

I'm not talking about being cold-hearted or running a military boot camp. I'm talking about helping children learn from all their experiences, bad as well as good. It is in times of struggle that we learn to be resilient, determined and open to new ideas. The philosopher, Fredrik Nietzsche, wrote: 'That which does not kill us makes us stronger.'[4] This may be too forceful in the context of children's learning. Perhaps the following quotes are more suitable:

Problems are to the mind what exercise is to the muscles: they toughen and make strong.

(Norman Vincent Peale, 1898–1993)[5]

The gem cannot be polished without friction, nor a person perfected without challenges.

(Chinese proverb)

A
Skills for learning
K

I recommend that as well as helping children develop learning attitudes, you should think about the skills children need for learning. Here's a list to begin with. It is not exhaustive but it will give you a reference point and underpins some of the activities later in the book.

Intellectual skills

Including the ability to:

- identify, describe and alter connections between ideas;
- understand the relevance of an idea;

- draw conclusions;
- compare and contrast;
- ask relevant questions;
- generate theories.

There are many suggestions for ways to develop these intellectual skills on pp. 61–71.

Social skills

Including the ability to:

- build rapport;
- respect other people's viewpoints;
- respond appropriately to others;
- work individually and in a team;
- encourage others;
- influence others.

Physical skills

Including the ability to:

- write, draw and paint;
- manipulate objects (e.g. building a model with *Lego*);
- catch and throw objects;
- dance, act, sing;
- balance and ride on a bike, horse, scooter;
- climb, sit still, play sport.

Communication skills

Including the ability to:

- understand and be understood;
- listen and respond appropriately to others;
- talk persuasively and respectfully;
- request things politely;
- pay full attention to a speaker;
- understand body language and tone of voice.

Of course, many of these skills overlap. Writing, painting and drawing are intellectual as well as physical skills. I've suggested some books and links on p. 14 that give more ideas for developing learning skills and attitudes with children. However, the most important thing is that you are thinking about and looking for ways to enhance children's attitudes and skills as well as their knowledge. By getting the balance right, you will give children a great head start.

A S
Knowledge for learning

National Curriculum documents identify the subject knowledge that a country wishes its young people to learn. Problems arise, however, if topics are then taught 'because they are in the curriculum' rather than because they are of interest to pupils.

One way to heighten the desire of pupils to learn particular bodies of knowledge is to use preview strategies.

As a teacher I would devote a small part of the week to previewing the topics we would cover in the following week. So, for example, I would say that we would begin a new topic on tourism and then ask pupils (a) what they *wanted* to know about tourism and (b) what they thought we *should* know about tourism by the end of the unit. We would then list the questions on the board, group them into units of work (or lesson plans) and, if there was time, begin some initial research.

There are many benefits to previewing, including:

1   Motivating children, who tend to be more engaged when they are involved in planning and making decisions about their own learning.

2   Giving children the opportunity to prepare themselves for lessons. Too frequently, children do not know what's coming up until the moment the lesson begins and their teacher outlines the learning objectives. Previewing allows children thinking time, opportunities to do some preparatory research and the possibility of approaching lessons in a prepared state of mind.

3   Helping parents to support their child's learning. I've lost count of the number of parents and grandparents who have thanked me as a teacher for previewing topics with their children. They say it has stimulated interesting discussions at home, led to more eagerness to visit the local library or online resource and provoked ideas for activities.

Motivation for learning

According to Jacqueline Eccles' *expectancy-value* theory,[6] the effort someone puts into a task is equal to how much they *want* to achieve it multiplied by how much they *expect* to achieve it.

Effort = value × expectancy

'Multiplied' is the key – since if either figure is zero (zero desire/value or zero expectancy) then the effort will also be zero, regardless of the other factor (since anything multiplied by zero is zero).

It is far better to focus on learning goals. This identifies the next step for an individual, regardless of where their peers are – for example, a two-year-old learning a handful of new words each week; a seven-year-old learning a new times table every other month; or ensuring that achieving 100 per cent in a test is a challenge for all students, not just some.

Top tips for learning *how* to learn

(a) Learning is a process, not an outcome

When teaching children something, take the opportunity to help them learn *how* to learn. For example:

> If you are teaching them to ride a bike, talk before and after about the attitudes (such as perseverance, concentration and having a go) needed for all types of learning, including learning to ride a bike.

> If you're helping them complete their homework, talk about the study or research skills that they might draw upon or improve while completing the assignment.

(b) Motivation, motivation, motivation

Effort = value × expectancy

As explored on the previous page, how much effort someone puts into a task is equal to how much they *want* to achieve it multiplied by how much they *expect* to achieve it.

It is important also to consider the benchmark we set for expectancy: are we aiming to be nothing short of the best, in which case our expectancy 'score' might be quite low; or are we aiming to beat our *personal* best, in which case our expectancy might be quite high.

(c) The attitude of learning

When observing or talking about someone's success, point out the role that attitudes have played. Of course, ability may well have played its part, but attitudes are likely to be a key influence.

To believe that they can succeed, children need to feel they can influence outcomes. Realising that the attitude they adopt may have an impact on the likelihood of success helps them to acquire an understanding of their own power to determine the outcome.

(d) Model it

Children mimic those around them. If you give the impression of knowing everything, then that is what the children around you will perceive is important. If, however, you show that you enjoy learning, are keen to learn from your mistakes and are willing to try new things, then the children around you are very likely to pick up on this and value learning too.

(e) Learning goals: 1/Performance targets: 0

Too often we set goals according to what is typical for an age group – for example, expecting all two-year-olds to be able to talk; all seven-year-olds to know their two, five and ten times tables; or all top-set maths students to achieve 100 per cent. These are *performance* goals.

It is far better to focus on where the individual child needs to go next, regardless of where their peers are. These are *learning* goals regardless of where their peers are – for example, helping all two-year-olds learn a handful of new words every week; seven-year-olds to learn a new times table every other month; or ensuring that achieving 100 per cent is a stretch for all students.

Further evidence

A common criticism of teaching children attitudes and skills, as well as knowledge, goes along the lines of: 'Why are you wasting time on personal and social skills lessons when children today don't even know their times tables?'

This creates an unnecessary polarisation. It is not a case of *either* teach skills and attitudes *or* knowledge.

Attitudes, skills and knowledge go hand in hand. Children who are unwilling (or unable) to persist with their studies or be open to help from others are going to struggle to learn anything, including their times tables.

Another criticism, this time levelled by teachers and school governors, is that because so much knowledge is needed to pass national tests, we shouldn't waste time developing skills and attitudes. The argument goes: 'If their parents haven't brought them up properly then what can or should we do about it? We're here to teach subjects, not attitudes!'

Though there may be some truth to this, it is also the case (as I will show in Chapter 4) that:

- to pass exams with the best grades, pupils need to have highly developed skills – particularly thinking skills;
- taking time to develop the right attitudes will mean less time wasted in dealing with low-level disruption and pupils unwilling to engage in activities.

Further reading and viewing

For further information about attitudes, skills and knowledge, I recommend:

Books

Building Learning Power by Guy Claxton, with his focus on the 4 'R's of 'Resilience, Resourcefulness, Reflectiveness and Reciprocity' (ISBN: 978–1901219432)

Challenging Learning by James Nottingham, a more comprehensive version of this book. (ISBN: 978–0956482808)

Teach Your Child to Think by Edward de Bono (ISBN: 014–126805)

People Rules for Rocket Scientists by Edwards *et al.* (ISBN: 978–1851686032)

What's the Point of School by Guy Claxton (ISBN: 064–6338005)

Videos

Child of Our Time website – excellent series from the BBC

Ted.com – particularly clips featuring Sir Ken Robinson or Dan Pink

YouTube – *Shift Happens* by Karl Fisch

Questionnaire

Here is a questionnaire that would be interesting to complete before moving on to the next chapter. It will help identify your beliefs about learning, intelligence, personality and growth – all of which are discussed in the next two chapters.

Reference to the answers you give can be found on p. 34.

QUESTIONNAIRE

		a	*b*	*c*	*d*
1	A person can change the way they act but they can't change their personality.	☐	☐	☐	☐
2	Intelligence is more to do with how you act than who you are.	☐	☐	☐	☐
3	I know how intelligent I am compared to those around me.	☐	☐	☐	☐
4	No matter who you are and how you act, you can always change your ways.	☐	☐	☐	☐
5	There are things I'm naturally good at and other things I'll never be able to do.	☐	☐	☐	☐
6	A person can change their personality a lot.	☐	☐	☐	☐
7	A person's moral character is something basic to them and they can't change it very much.	☐	☐	☐	☐
8	I like to learn even if it means making mistakes in front of other people.	☐	☐	☐	☐
9	Shy people will always be shy and confident people will always be confident.	☐	☐	☐	☐
10	I get more pleasure from beating my personal best than I do from being better than others.	☐	☐	☐	☐
11	If I knew I wasn't going to do very well at something, I probably wouldn't do it even if I might learn from it.	☐	☐	☐	☐
12	The more you learn, the more intelligent you become.	☐	☐	☐	☐

a	b	c	d
Strongly agree	Agree	Disagree	Strongly disagree

2

How talented are your children?

The willingness to invest in learning, to gain a reputation as a learner, and to show openness to experiences are the key dispositional factors that relate to achievement.

(John Hattie, 2009)[7]

FIGURE 2.1 Multi-talented child

Introduction

I noticed a young man at the back of a maths class recently who was flailing his arms around frenetically. All the other students were paying full attention to the teacher. This went on for the whole lesson. Afterwards I asked the teacher whether this was normal, to which she replied, rather proudly: 'Damian is a kinaesthetic learner – he learns better when he moves.'

What a load of rubbish! The boy doesn't have a medical condition: he's simply been told he's a kinaesthetic learner and gone along with it because it sounds fun. His teacher had asked her students to complete a learning styles questionnaire and then concluded that some were visual learners, others were auditory and the rest were kinaesthetic. She'd gone on to declare that visual learners had to see something written down to learn well; auditory learners had to hear something; and the kinaesthetic lot – well, they had to bop and groove to learn!

Don't get me wrong: I agree we all have preferences. I seem to remember things better if I've seen them written down but it's not *impossible* for me to learn through listening, despite what my wife would tell you.

However, herein lies a problem: so many people seem to believe that they'll *always* be good at certain things and therefore *never* any good at other things that they tend to steer clear of anything they're not 'naturally' good at. How often, for example, might a father say: 'Don't ask me, I was never any good at spelling – go and ask your mother!' What this implies to the child is: 'Aha, so there's a genetic reason I can't spell: I have a clay-brained father. There's no point in trying because I'll always be bad at spelling.'

Howard Gardner explored this theme at a conference I was also speaking at in 2009 in Kuala Lumpur. He began his keynote speech by saying he wished teachers had never come across his theory of multiple intelligences because so many of them were obsessed with categorising kids. An interesting opening line for a speech attended by more than 1,000 teachers!

Gardner's theory of multiple intelligences proposes that instead of one general form of intelligence, typically measured by IQ tests, there could be as many as eight intelligences (or nine if you include the existential/spiritual intelligence he has recently been considering):

- spatial (ability to visualise);
- linguistic (language skills);
- logical–mathematical (abstract/logical thought);
- bodily–kinaesthetic (dexterity);
- interpersonal (understanding others);
- intrapersonal (self awareness);
- musical (sensitivity to pitch, rhythm, timbre);
- naturalistic (sensitivity to nature).

Though responses to Gardner's theory have been mixed, it continues to be used (and misused) in schools around the world. As inspiration for a wider range of activities in lessons, the theory has many benefits. However, using it in the way our friend with a learning styles questionnaire did is nonsensical.

Setting tasks for children based on their horoscope wouldn't be tolerated: strict guidelines for the Capricorns, no rules for the Sagittarians and plenty of quiet activities for the shy Pisceans. So it has to be wondered why some teachers set tasks according to which of the eight multiple intelligences students have scored most highly on.

Not that adults outside of schools are immune to such silly behaviour. How many times have you heard things said similar to the following?

Child: 'I hate maths. I can't do it.'

Adult: 'But you're very talented at painting.' (This has the potential to suggest: 'I agree that you're no good at maths but don't worry about that; focus on your strengths instead.')

'Why can't you be more like your sister?' (*Message*: 'She has talents or attitudes you don't have and probably never will have.')

'I know you only got six out of ten in your science test, but you did well in your history exam.' (*Inference*: 'There's nothing you can do to improve your science performance so just concentrate on doing well in history again.')

'Her brother is the clever one of the family; she's the more social one.' (This is problematic because there's a risk of defining and therefore probably predetermining, the skills each child will excel at and which they'll always struggle with.)

The problem with all of the example comments is that they imply skills and talents are fixed. Saying 'never mind about one thing because you'll be more successful with another' suggests that everyone would be better off ignoring their weaknesses and focussing on their strengths. This might be wise advice for job seekers but what if a child is struggling with their language skills? Should we say: 'Never mind, plenty of people get by with poor literacy skills' or should we help them set learning goals (see p. 13) and make progress?

Indeed, the following summary accompanied research led by Professor Cathy Price of the Wellcome Trust Centre for Neuroimaging at University College London (published in *Nature*, October 2011):

Our results emphasise the possibility that an individual's intellectual capacity relative to their peers can decrease or increase in the teenage years. This would be encouraging to those whose intellectual potential may improve, and would be a warning that early achievers may not maintain their potential.

Some of you might be thinking, 'But some people really are Tim, Tim, nice but dim' or 'What about the Einsteins of the world? They obviously *are* more intelligent than most.'

I've been purposefully skirting around this issue until now because I know how strongly people hold beliefs about the origins of intelligence and talents, but here goes. . . .

Does ability come from nature or nurture?

Does ability come from nature or nurture? If you've thought about this before then you've probably already made up your mind and there's nothing I can say to change it. However, please bear with me because I'd like to show you that what you *believe* makes a BIG difference to whether you're more likely to help or to hinder children's learning.

I think I can say, without controversy, that both nature and nurture play their role in determining intelligence and talents. But what is the balance between the two?

In 2011, I gave a keynote address at a conference in Invercargill, New Zealand. The weekend previously, I'd broken three ribs skiing so I wasn't looking forward to it. Thankfully, the welcome from the teachers in the town was as warm as I've experienced so I was buoyed up and ready to go. Then the first presenter, a multi-award winning speaker, began with the 'fact' that intelligence is 60 per cent nature and 40 per cent nurture.

How could she be so sure? What research did she base this claim on? Or was it a convenient 'truth' that allowed her to concentrate her presentation on the nature of people?

As far as I'm aware, there is no such verifiable statistic and how could there be? Intelligence and talents are based on so many variables. I've studied many research papers and books on the subject (see p. 29 for a list of the best books on the subject) but cannot find anyone willing to make such a claim. Here, though, are some examples to muddy the waters still further:

- *Wolfgang Mozart* is thought of as a genius or, at the very least, a prodigious talent. However, his father Leopold was also a composer, a leading figure of the court orchestra in Vienna and an accomplished music teacher who presented both the young son and his sister at several musical exhibitions across Europe. Was Wolfgang's talent natural or significantly developed?

- *Sir Bobby Charlton* had four uncles who played professional football (Jack, George, Jim and Stan) and his mother's cousin, Jackie Milburn, is one of the most celebrated footballers ever to have played for Newcastle United. Together with his brother Jack, Bobby starred in the World Cup winning team of 1966. Not a bad gene pool I'd say! However, what influence would the following also have had on the development of this former European footballer of the year?

(a) The Charlton brothers were the only young lads in Ashington to have a real football to play with (regularly donated by one of their professional footballing uncles).

(b) Older boys in the town were always willing to let Bobby play with them so long as he brought his real, leather football with him.

(c) Bobby credits his mother, Cissie, for her role in his development. Almost unheard of for a woman in a mining town in the 1940s, Cissie knew the game of football intimately and coached many of the local boys' teams as well as her sons.

(d) When Bobby watched a game, he'd have one or more of his uncles next to him using the opportunity to offer extra coaching. 'I'd watch Stanley Matthews and wonder what made him better than anyone else. My uncles said, just watch his first ten yards. After that I practised sprinting with my granddad, who trained professional sprinters.'[8] At the peak of his game, there was no one quicker over ten yards than Bobby Charlton.

■ *Sir Richard Branson* has dyslexia and performed relatively poorly academically. However, his parents always encouraged him to strive for his goals and supported his risk-taking, even as a pupil at Stowe school when he began his first business, the *Student* magazine. Today his Virgin Group is made up of more than 400 companies.

■ *Dame Evelyn Glennie* was the first professional solo percussionist in the Western world. This is despite being profoundly deaf since the age of twelve.

■ *Tiger Woods* was introduced to golf before the age of two by his father, Earl. Woods senior would practise his golf swing while Woods junior copied him, from his highchair. Makes me wonder whether it's too late to get my own son into golf now he's already three!

I realise the examples I have given do not account for the broad spectrum of human endeavour. However, I think this is a reflection on what we celebrate and therefore know about in society, rather than any oversight on my part. After all, how many competitions regularly identify the best teachers, bankers, nurses, or even geographers?

Regardless of the limited range of examples, my point is that even the most 'natural' of talents seems to have benefited considerably from early and sustained advantages that helped nurture their abilities.

I'm not saying that I'll ever be able to run as fast as Paula Radcliffe but does that mean I should never enter a marathon? Or just because I'm unlikely ever to influence Western thinking in the way Albert Einstein has, should I therefore steer

bright	average	slow
clever kids	middle set	strugglers
top set	middle kids	bottom set
gifted and talented	plodders	non-academic
genius	normal	special needs
academic	typical	remedial

JNP

FIGURE 2.2 Labels and stereotypes

clear of maths or physics? Of course not! And yet it is alarming how many times people say: 'Some kids just aren't made for numbers' or 'Bless him, he'll never set the world alight but at least he's a friendly fella.'

One day in July 2010, I was preparing for a lesson that would be observed by a group of teachers. Imagine my dismay when the teenagers I was going to work with walked in and their teacher told me: 'These are not the bright ones.' Dismayed by this comment but not deterred, I began the lesson by asking the students what they were studying. 'VCAL', they told me. I asked them what that meant. 'It's the Victoria Certificate of Applied Learning. Basically, it means we're dumb. The bright ones do VCE but if you're dumb like us then you learn how to use your hands and do VCAL.' I wish I could tell you I was making this up to illustrate a point but I'm not. This really happened. The kids were only sixteen yet this was how they viewed themselves.

Appalled though most teachers are at this story, it is still common for schools to label children as either bright or average or as having special needs, as if intelligence was constant regardless of context or type of challenge. Indeed, one college in Greenwich, south London, has gone further than that and created three separate spaces for the different 'categories' of ability – complete with different uniforms, buildings, teachers, play areas and lunchtimes.[9]

Fans of the 11-plus or grammar school system may well see nothing wrong with this. Chris Woodhead, ex-chief inspector of schools, would no doubt support the idea, as he claims that a child's 'genes are likely to be better if their parents are teachers, academics, lawyers'. He has also called for more segregation by ability to 'prevent average pupils dragging down more intelligent classmates'.[10]

Pernicious though I think this is, I am not suggesting that all children have the same abilities. Of course they don't. But I don't believe genes account for the difference to the degree Woodhead believes. Children from middle class families often perform better at school but surely this has as much to do with advantages of stability, extra-curricular activities, language used in the home, and so on, as it has to do with genes?

In the 1960s, two professors from Kansas City, Betty Hart and Todd Risley, found the average vocabulary of three-year-olds varied as follows:

- 1,116 words for children with professional parents;
- 749 words for children with working class parents;
- 525 words for children with welfare-dependent parents.[11]

At first glance, this might seem to support Woodhead's theory. However, what Hart and Risley also found was professional parents spoke over 2,000 words per hour to their children, working class parents spoke about 1,300 and parents who were welfare-dependent spoke about 600 words. That's a considerable difference in opportunity – or nurture – for each group of children!

More recent research from the Rowntree Foundation (2010) found that some children begin school in the UK with a working vocabulary of 6,000 words, whereas others begin with just 500.

Let's imagine that over the next 12 months you spend 100 hours with fluent Arabic speakers and develop a working vocabulary of 6,000 words; I spend the same number of hours but with non-Arabic speakers who do their best to help me learn approximately 500 words of Arabic. After the 12 months, we both start formal Arabic lessons. Guess which one of us is more likely to perform at a higher level at the start of those lessons?

However, what would you think of the suggestion that we should be labelled before we start those formal lessons? I'll probably be labelled *average* and taught in one group whereas you'll probably be labelled *gifted and talented* and taught in another. How would you feel about that? Bear in mind, you'll probably have more expected of you; you'll be stretched and challenged by your teachers, because that's what is expected of the gifted and talented. As for me, well I'm average, so unless I really intend to push myself forward and stand out from the crowd then I'll be given work that is 'average'.

How fair does that seem?

> Some recent philosophers have given their moral approval to the deplorable verdict that an individual's intelligence is a fixed quantity, one which cannot be augmented. We must protest and act against this brutal pessimism . . . it has no foundation whatsoever.
>
> (Alfred Binet, 1909)[12]

Intelligence testing

In 1904, Alfred Binet was asked by the French government to create a mechanism for identifying students in need of alternative education. Note the emphasis: not for students who were clever or stupid, but for students who the curriculum did not suit so that an alternative one could be developed for them.

Binet created a scale of thirty tasks for six- to fourteen-year-olds, ranging from easy to complex ones. When he published the results, he stressed the limitations of his scale. He emphasised that intellect developed at variable rates, could be influenced by the environment, was malleable rather than fixed and could only be compared between children from comparable backgrounds.[13]

However, at the same time over the Atlantic, there was a focus on creating the 'American Dream' – leaving the old aristocracies of Europe behind and building a meritocracy. The problem was, this dream was only available to white people – black African slaves were not invited. Which is why, when Binet's work was translated into English, it was adapted culturally and philosophically so that it could be used to 'prove' the higher intelligence of white people.

Binet's response to the 'foreign ideas being grafted on his instrument' was to condemn those who with 'brutal pessimism' and 'deplorable verdicts' were promoting the concept of intelligence as a single, unitary construct.[14]

Indeed, consider this. If I were to ask how healthy you are, what would you take into account? How much exercise you've taken recently? How well you sleep? Whether you've endured any serious illnesses? Your frame of mind? Even your social life? There are so many factors to consider that it seems almost ridiculous to suggest you could rate your health on a scale of 0–10; even more so to suggest that the score would remain constant throughout your life.

This is comparable to the claims made about intelligence – that it can be easily quantified and that it remains pretty constant throughout one's life. How very silly! Yet it is this belief that leads us to compare and label varying degrees of intelligence – from 'gifted' to 'average' to the apparently 'not intelligent'.

Interestingly, Lewis Terman – the psychologist who led the adaptation of Binet's work – was a prominent eugenicist. When he published the Stanford-Binet IQ test, he wrote:

> High-grade or borderline deficiency . . . is very, very common among Spanish-Indian and Mexican families of the Southwest and also among negroes. Their dullness seems to be racial, or at least inherent in the family stocks from which they come. . . . Children of this group should be segregated into separate classes. . . . They cannot master abstractions but they can often be made into efficient workers . . . from a eugenic point of view they constitute a grave problem because of their unusually prolific breeding.[15]

What's the right way to group children?

Schools typically have too many children and too few teachers. Having a class of 25–35 children with wildly different interests, competences and attitudes is far from an ideal setting for learning. That said, how many taxpayers would agree to doubling the education budget so that class sizes could be halved? And, given the number of commentators who accuse teachers of having an easy ride and of not generating any wealth for the country, I wonder whether enough extra teachers could be recruited even if the funding was available?

FIGURE 2.3 Abilities and groupings

So that leaves us with a decision to make: how should we group children? Should it be by 'year of manufacture'? If you were born between September one year and August the next (as it is in England) then you'll be in the same class at school, regardless of the fact that the September baby will have had 11 months more time to develop before starting school than his August-born classmate.

So how about grouping by ability? This is very common in many of the countries I work in – Australia, New Zealand, USA, the UK – but quite rare in the Scandinavian countries I visit. Unfortunately, though, the research around ability grouping is unclear.

In a systematic review of fifty-one studies into within-class grouping of children by ability, Yiping Lou and her colleagues found that ability grouping *can* have

Effect size

An effect size is one way to compare results that were originally measured on different scales. While some studies in education report in terms of national exam scores, others refer to teacher-made tests or graded coursework. There are also some studies that are short-term whereas others involve longitudinal data collected over many years. Thus to improve the validity of any comparison between these studies, it is useful to convert the data to an effect size.

Professor John Hattie is responsible for the most comprehensive study to date, having analysed more than 60,000 studies and sorted them according to their effect size.

Hattie's conclusion is that the average effect size is 0.4

Anything more than 0.4 represents a significantly-positive effect on pupil achievement; anything between 0.4 and 0.0 is positive but less than average and anything below 0.0 represents a negative effect on pupil achievement.

> If we set the bar at zero and then ask that teachers and schools 'improve achievement', we have set a very low bar indeed. No wonder every teacher can claim they are making a difference; no wonder we can find many answers as to how to enhance achievement. ... Enhancing learning beyond an effect size of $d = 0.0$ is so low a bar as to be dangerous and misleading. Set the bar at $d = 0.4$. The average effect size is $d = 0.4$. This average summarizes the typical effect of all possible influences in education and should be used as the benchmark to judge effects in education.
>
> (Hattie, 2009)[16]

a positive effect when compared with no grouping at all but it tends to have a negative effect on lower-ability children.

Meta-analyses of the sort completed by Lou *et al.*, generally report impact in terms of average effect Size. This allows comparisons to be made along a standard scale rather than one study referring, for example, to the improvements in children's reading age while another references scores in maths tests.

Bearing in mind we're looking for an effect size in excess of 0.4, here are the results Lou and her colleagues found:

Ability grouping (general)	0.17
High ability students	0.09
Medium ability students	0.51
Low ability students	−0.60[17]

This shows that the gain for high-ability children is so small as to be almost worthless while the effect on low-ability children is damagingly negative. The only children who seemingly gain from ability grouping are the medium ability students. Possible reasons for this will be explored in the next chapter when I look at why we should avoid praising children for being bright, clever or intelligent.

So what's the answer to grouping children, given that ability grouping has mixed results at best? According to Robert Marzano's meta-analyses of hundreds of studies examining the options, he suggests that mixed-ability classes that are then divided into small cooperative learning groups are the best way forward.

From his book, *Classroom Instruction that Works*, he states: 'Organizing students in cooperative learning groups has a powerful effect on learning (effect size 0.78).'[18] He explains further that:

- Organising groups based on ability levels should be used sparingly.
- Cooperative groups should be kept to pairs or at the most groups of 3–4.
- Cooperative learning should be applied consistently and systematically, but not overused. For example, one way to vary the grouping patterns would be to have:
  - informal groups (e.g., talk partners, turn to your neighbour and share a question/idea/connection);
  - formal groups that are set for the completion of a task over a number of days or weeks and include individual and group accountability;
  - base groups that stick together for a term or a year and complete a range of planned, informal and social tasks together.

So what does this mean if you are a parent or grandparent who doesn't have the responsibility of organising large groups of children at school, Brownies, sports clubs or similar? The lesson is that variety is the key.

Your children (or grandchildren) will learn most when they experience a mix of working by themselves, working informally with one or two other children, and working also as part of more formal group of mixed age and ability children to complete a project together.

Thus, if we can encourage them to get involved in different activities and clubs with different children of different ages, then our children are most likely to learn more.

Who needed to know about *effect sizes* to know that?!

A cautionary note about collaborative groups

It is easy to get carried away with the idea that teamwork or cooperative groups are among the best ways to learn. Sadly, this is simply not true: sometimes the desire to achieve consensus and work together amiably can lead to a disregard for critical thinking. This is sometimes referred to as *Groupthink*.

Signs that cooperative groups might be sacrificing thoughtfulness for the sake of efficiency include:

- *Overestimation of the group* – members see themselves as infallible, as well as superior to all other groups.

- *Intolerance* – members tend to reject any outside views that do not fit with their own. They also create, or draw attention to, negative stereotypes of others.

- *Pressure to conform* – within the team, there is a strong intolerance for differing opinions. Members with dissenting views are pressured to protect the status quo.

Before reading the next chapter, may I suggest you look back at the questionnaire on p. 15 and decide if there are any of your answers you'd like to change?

Top tips for developing talents

1   Focus on learning not labelling

Avoid using labels such as visual learner, naturally talented, or hopeless speller. Instead focus on learning and say things such as 'I'd love the chance to improve my spelling', or 'I remember things more if I see them so I'm having a go at learning by listening and doing'.

2   Say 'I'd like to improve'

If we say we've never been good at something then it gives the impression that we believe that's the way it always was and therefore always will be. Instead, demonstrate or talk about the things you are trying to improve.

Mention your motivation for learning, your trials and tribulations along the way and your joy at making progress. In other words, show you are a learner too!

3　If grouping children, go for fluidity

When I worked with Professor Dweck (see Chapter 3), I heard her say again and again: 'If we label children, we limit them.' So avoid putting children into groups that suggest a 'label' – for example, always seating the highest achievers on a 'top table' or placing those who have been behind up until now in 'the bottom group', as if they have no chance of catching up. Instead, use cooperative groups and keep swapping them around so the focus becomes learning rather than labels.

Further reading

If you're interested in effect size comparisons in education then I recommend:

Classroom Instruction That Works by Robert Marzano, Debra Pickering and Jane Pollock. (ISBN: 978–0871205049)

Visible Learning for Teachers by John Hattie (ISBN: 978–0415690157)

For books about grouping children, go for:

Active Learning through Formative Assessment by Shirley Clarke (ISBN: 978–0340974452)

Gifted and Talented Pocketbook by Barry Hymer (ISBN: 978–1906610012)

Learning Without Limits by Susan Hart, Annabelle Dixon, Mary Ann Drummond and Donald Mcintyre (ISBN: 978–0335212590)

For books about intelligence, go for:

Brain Rules by John Medina (ISBN: 978–0979777745)

Intelligence and Intelligence Testing by Richard B. Fletcher and John Hattie (ISBN: 978–0415600927)

Self-theories: Their role in motivation, personality, and development by Carol Dweck (ISBN: 978–1841690247)

3

Don't call them gifted!

If you want to help children learn then here are some phrases to AVOID saying:

The child is a genius!
You're gifted.
Bright boy.
Clever girl.
You're a natural.
What a great reader.
You're by far the best.

FIGURE 3.1 Award-winning child

Introduction

If we tell children they are gifted, bright, clever, a natural or any of the other labels listed on p. 31, then we are in danger of suggesting their success is down to a 'natural' intelligence they have been given. On the face of it, this might be okay, but consider what these same children might think if they begin to fail: 'I can't be as clever, bright or gifted as I thought I was.' And: 'If my success is down to my level of intelligence, then surely my failures must be down to the same thing.'

As I will show you in this chapter, it is far better to use phrases such as:

> 'The child has some great ideas!' (*not 'the child is a genius'*)
>
> 'You're making wonderful progress!' (*not 'you're gifted'*)
>
> 'Bright idea!' (*not 'bright boy'*)
>
> 'Clever suggestion!' *(not 'clever girl')*
>
> 'Great skill' (*not 'you're a natural'*)
>
> 'What great reading!' (*not 'what a great reader'*)

All of the positive phrases focus on actions and thinking. They tell children that success (and therefore also failure) is due to behaviour. And of course behaviour is much easier to modify than intelligence is.

One way to decide which way to praise is to consider what the children might say to themselves if they begin to struggle. For example, if we say 'clever children' when they are doing well then how many of them might suspect that they are 'stupid children' when the going gets tough? Whereas if we say 'clever idea' then, even in their darkest moments, they are only going to end up saying they've had a 'stupid idea' (which seems less damming than 'I am stupid'.)

Which 'type' best describes you?

Type F

- You know you can learn new things but that won't really change how intelligent you are.
- There are some things you have always been good at and other things you'll never be able to do.
- There are some people you know who are naturally gifted.

Type G

- You believe that the more you learn, the more intelligent you become.
- You think you've developed your talents through your own endeavours and that your weaknesses are just waiting to be improved.
- You think the people who excel at certain things do so because of all their dedication and effort.

If your thinking is more in line with Type F then please, please, please read the following few pages very carefully because this type of thinking leads to behaviour that often gets in the way of learning.

If your thinking is more in line with Type G, then great – but don't rest on your laurels just yet! We're all prone to using phrases that don't help learning. So read on. . . .

NB. On p. 32, I explain the significance of 'Type F' and 'Type G' (rather than Type 'A' or 'B'.)

When people believe that their intelligence is more or less constant throughout their lives then this can cause them to:

- worry about how much intelligence they have;
- focus on showing that they are more intelligent than others;
- choose to do things that are easy for them so that they look clever;
- avoid any setback or challenge, or try to steer clear of people whom they perceive to be more intelligent.

These behaviours would be typical of 'Type F' people, as identified above.

However, when people believe that intelligence is not something they merely possess but something that can be enhanced through learning, then they tend to:

- focus on learning and improving;
- choose things that will stretch and challenge them;
- seek ways to put their knowledge to good use;
- look for what they can learn from mistakes and from more proficient people.

These behaviours would be typical of 'Type G' people, although please note that type G people don't deny there are differences between how much people know or how quickly they seem to master something. It's just that they focus on the idea that everyone can learn, given the right coaching, support, effort and time. Type F people, however, tend to focus on determining who is the smartest.

> It has become a common practice to praise students for their performance on easy tasks, to tell them they are smart when they do something quickly and perfectly. When we do this we are not teaching them to welcome challenge and learn from errors. We are teaching them that easy success means they are intelligent and, by implication, that errors and effort mean they are not.
>
> (Carol Dweck, 2000, Professor of Psychology, Stanford University)[19]

Fixed and growth mindsets

Carol Dweck, upon whose work I draw deeply and with whom I had the great pleasure of working in June 2010, has researched this topic in depth in her role as Professor of Psychology at Stanford University. She has found that some people believe their success is based on innate ability and says these people have a *fixed* theory of intelligence. Other people believe their success is based on hard work and learning. Dweck says these people have a *growth* or incremental theory of intelligence.

From the previous pages, Type F are those with a fixed mindset, whereas Type G are those with a growth mindset.

We might not necessarily be aware of our own mindset. However, our behaviour, our thinking and our comments tend to give us away.

Fixed mindset

These are the typical beliefs and attitudes of people with a fixed mindset:

Beliefs

- Intelligence and ability are *fixed*.
- *Nature* determines intelligence and ability.
- I will always be good at some things (e.g. maths) and poor at other things (e.g. art).

Priorities

- *Prove* myself.
- Succeed, especially with little effort, as this proves I am clever.
- Avoid failure of any sort.

Responses to challenges

- Blame myself or, to protect my ego, blame someone else.
- *Feel inferior* or incapable.
- Try guessing the answers or copying others.
- Seek ego-boosting distractions.

Mottos

- Either you're good at something or you're not.
- If you're really good at something, you shouldn't need to try.
- *If you have to try, you must be stupid.*
- Don't try too hard; that way you've got an excuse if things go wrong.
- No pain, no pain!

Growth mindset

These are the typical beliefs and attitudes of people with a growth mindset:

Beliefs

- Intelligence and ability can *grow*.
- *Nurture* determines intelligence and ability.
- If I apply myself more, seek help, take risks, change my strategy, then I've got a good chance of learning anything.

Priorities

- *Improve* myself.
- Learn through challenge, as this will help me to grow my talents.
- Seek interesting challenges that will stretch and help me to learn.

Responses to challenges

- There is no blame – I just want to know how to do it better next time.
- *Feel inspired* to have a go.
- Try various problem-solving strategies.
- Seek advice, support or new strategies.

Mottos

- Success comes with application.
- No matter how good you are at something, you can always improve.
- *If you have to try, you must be learning.*
- Always try hard; that way you've more chance of success and making progress.
- No pain, no gain!

Take a look at your answers to the questionnaire on p. 15. If you answered with more a's and b's on questions 1, 3, 5, 7, 9, 11 or c's and d's on the even numbered questions then you may well have a fixed mindset.

As Dweck shows clearly in her books *Mindset: The new psychology of success*, (2006) and *Self-theories: Their role in motivation, personality and development* (1999) and I show over the next few pages, a growth mindset is far more likely to improve learning and thus to help children learn.

A connection between mindset and praise

One of the best introductions to Dweck's work comes from an article she wrote with Claudia Mueller for the *Journal of Personality and Social Psychology* in 1998. In it they describe a series of six tests they did to discover the effect of praise on children's performance.[20]

The first test involved 128 ten- and eleven-year-olds (seventy girls and fifty-eight boys, aged ten–twelve years). Each child was seen individually by one of four experimenters. After being escorted from their usual classroom to an empty one, they were introduced to the task. They were given a brief guide to problem solving and then asked to solve ten moderately difficult questions in four minutes.

As soon as the time was up, the adult marked their tests and told the child he/she had done well:

> Wow, you did very well on these problems. You got [number of problems] right. That's a really high score.

Regardless of their actual score, all children were told that they had solved at least 80 per cent of the questions they had answered.

Each child then received one of three types of praise, as follows:

Approximately one-third of the children were given *Intelligence Praise* – they were told they had done well 'because they were clever'.

Approximately one-third of the children were given *Process Praise* – they were told they had done well 'because they had tried hard'.

Approximately one-third of the children were the *control group* – they were told they had done well but given no further explanation as to why.

Each child was then given another test, this time far more difficult. Every child struggled.

They were then told they had performed 'a lot worse' on the second test than on the first test. (See Note p. 38.)

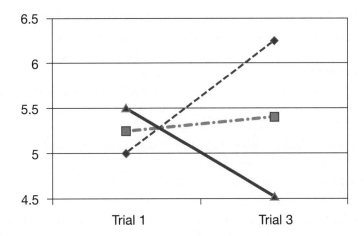

FIGURE 3.2 Graph showing children's test scores

After receiving this negative feedback, each child was asked to work on the third and final set of problems. These were of the same standard as the first set (moderate difficulty) so it could be reasonably expected that each child would have got the same score as they had on the first test. Except they didn't.

The graph in Figure 3.2 shows how the children's scores changed from the first set of problems to the third set of problems, after receiving the different types of praise.

The numbers down the left show the average score out of ten achieved by the groups of children:

Black line – children who received intelligence praise.

Broken line – children who received process praise.

Dot and dash line – children in the control group.

As you will see from the graph:

- The children who were praised for being clever did worse on the third test than they had on the first test.
- The children who were praised for having tried hard did better on the third test than they had on the first test.
- The children in the control group did slightly better over time, probably because they were getting used to taking the tests.

I often quote this research when I'm giving a keynote address at conferences. After presenting the graph, I ask volunteers to suggest reasons why praising children for being clever could have such a negative impact. The most common suggestions are:

- If children are told they are clever, they might then rest on their laurels.

- When the children struggled in the second test, those who had been praised for being clever might have questioned whether they had been lied to about being clever.

- There is a common assumption that if you are clever then you should never struggle. Thus, when the children struggled with the second test, they decided they were not clever.

- Those children who believed they were clever decided the tests were stupid and that they did not need to prove themselves.

- 'Clever' children are more likely to suspect the test is a trick used to catch them out.

- Children who receive intelligence praise feel threatened by tasks they can't do and so give up, whereas children who get process praise often feel prompted to try even harder.

All these suggestions are likely to have some truth to them, particularly as they are based mainly on experienced teachers' and parents' observations of how 'clever' children respond to success and failure.

I would add one more to the list: the differing degrees to which children believe they can make the changes necessary to improve their performance.

When the children given intelligence praise struggled in the second test, what strategies were open to them? Unless they could whip out a bigger brain or take an intelligence pill, they may well have believed they were powerless to improve their scores.

Conversely, those children who had been praised for effort presumably thought: 'I must try harder', since that is what they had been told generates high scores.

To be successful in learning, children need to know that their actions influence outcomes. They should realise that they've succeeded *because* of their efforts, not just because they were 'given' the ability by their genes.

Note about the test conditions

During the debriefing given at the end of the experimental session, all children were informed that the second problem set contained problems of increased difficulty, which were considered to be appropriate for students who were two years older. In fact, they were told that answering even one of these difficult problems was quite an achievement for students in their grade level. Thus, they were assured of the overall high quality of their task performance. Extensive precautions were taken to ensure that all children left the experimental setting proud of their performance (Mueller and Dweck, 1998).[21]

This is where the key to positive praise lies:

> If we praise children for something they have control over (effort, focus, determination and so on) then we empower them to learn and grow.

> If we praise them for something they assume they been 'given' (such as cleverness, a 'natural' talent, a gift, and so on) then we may inadvertently cause them to believe they have no influence over their successes and failures.

Supporting the conclusions from this research does not mean I am a parent who is impossible to please, or one that never gives praise for fear of spoiling the child.

Interestingly, most parents seem to accept that it is much better to criticise bad behaviour than it is to criticise their child. Saying 'that was a naughty thing to do' is far more preferable than saying 'you're a naughty child'. I would say it works the same way with praise: it is better to say 'that was a clever thing to do' than to say 'you're a clever child'.

Children who believe their successes are due to their own efforts and endeavours tend to be more willing to learn.

Children who believe their successes are due to 'being clever' are more inclined to show off what they know and to stick to activities they know they can excel at.

Over the next few pages you will find a further exploration of praise. If you have any questions, please post them on encouraginglearning.com and I will endeavour to answer them as best as I can.

FIGURE 3.3 The gift of a bigger brain

> One of the most damaging aspects of the 'gift' mentality is that it makes us think we can know in advance who has the gift. This, I believe, is what makes us try to identify groups who have it and groups who don't – as in, 'boys have it and girls don't, or those who show early promise have it and others don't.
>
> (Dweck, 2012)[22]

What's wrong with gifts?

In April 2010, I was heading for my plane home from Copenhagen when ash from an Icelandic volcano forced the closure of the airport. For ten hours I sat in one of the lounges and waited. Opposite me was a father and a son. The boy can't have been more than four or five years old and yet for the whole ten hours they played chess.

Unusual though this might be, my point is that I bet there are a number of teachers, parents, or classmates at the boy's school who refer to him as being a *gifted* chess player. Despite the (presumably) hundreds of hours he has spent learning to play the game, all the effort, all the challenges, he is referred to as gifted – as if he was *given* his talent.

You see, 'gifts' suggest that a person's ability has been bestowed upon them. It disregards all the blood, sweat and tears that have been shed in developing the talent: the hundreds of hours that the boy spent playing chess; the dedication and practice Tiger Woods has put into his golf; the trial and error Evelyn Glennie went through to teach herself how to 'feel' rather than hear music.

I'm not saying that 'gift' or 'gifted' are bad words but I would suggest, as my friend and colleague Professor Barry Hymer advises, that you think in terms of 'gift-creation'.[23] By this he means it is better to help children *grow* gifts rather than pouring our energies into identifying and labelling their gifts. Or, as he so beautifully put it in an email to a friend:

> What drives us in our society to pin children to their measured competencies, like so many dried and mounted butterflies? Let's enjoy their colours, not measure them. Let's not pin them down – let's watch them in flight.
>
> (Barry Hymer, 2007)

Gifts from God

I realise many people believe our talents are indeed gifts from God. When I was younger many of my more religious friends would encourage me to remark that we are *blessed*, not lucky, when things go our way.

However, I don't think this viewpoint is necessarily in opposition to a *growth* view of praise. After all, isn't there a duty to make the most of our gifts or to 'honour God' by nurturing and using wisely the gifts He has given us?

My child really *is* a genius

After I'd made a presentation to parents at a school near Bondi Beach recently, a mother approached me and boasted: 'My son's a genius.' Apparently, her son was working at the level of children five years his senior and was achieving perfect scores in several subjects.

The next day, I met her son, who was eight. Despite this, he had apparently read as many books in his short life as I had in my whole childhood. Perhaps he was a genius after all?

But then the lesson began.

As the children and I wondered why it was okay to make up stories but not to tell lies, the boy became increasingly agitated. He resented not knowing the 'right' answer before anyone else and responded to every question as if it were a personal criticism. Before long, he was trying out all sorts of distracting behaviour, hoping to bring the lesson back to the safe territory of facts and right or wrong answers.

After the lesson, I found out some background information. He is an only child living with two parents and four grandparents. He has a voracious appetite for knowledge, perhaps created, but certainly encouraged, by the adults in his life. The only out-of-school activities he does are fact-based – no sports clubs, social activities or music lessons. Of course, far be it for me to say how he should spend his time – but that's not the question. The question is whether the boy is a genius or not, or even whether geniuses exist.

This reminds me of another encounter I had in Australia. I was working with a primary school near Melbourne when one of the teachers remarked that none of his Vietnamese pupils could catch a ball, even by the time they left school aged eleven. I asked why he thought this might be, to which he replied: 'Perhaps it's something genetic?'

'What's their level of English like?' I asked. 'Better than any of our Aussie kids!' he replied. 'How about their maths?' 'Oh, I reckon they're geniuses – the lot of them.'

Can this really be true: that Vietnamese children growing up in Australia are all blessed with numeracy and literacy genes but no sporting genes? Or might it have something to do with spending most of their waking hours on extra study, attending Vietnamese school at weekends and having parents who are determined to ensure their children make the most of the opportunities their new country presents? I know it's almost abhorrent to an Aussie that a child wouldn't have any interest in sport but there are only so many hours in the day and if these are spent studying then there's not a lot of time for games.

Don't get me wrong – I'm not making fun of Australia. I delight in working with the warm and fantastically friendly people I find there. Perhaps it's their honesty and self-deprecating humour that allows me to unearth more stories than I typically find in other, more reserved, countries.

The mindset of boys vs. girls

It might not surprise you to know that boys tend to receive more criticism than girls – as much as eight times more, according to Dweck.[24]

However, what you might find more surprising is that girls tend to suffer more because of it.

Allow me to explain: I do a lot of work with pre-schools. Whenever I visit these wonderful places of learning, I can't help noticing that the girls are more likely to be engaged in nice, neat, tidy, social play – and being praised for it – whereas the boys are more likely to be making a mess or being rough with each other – and being criticised for it.

This doesn't happen only in pre-schools but it does tend to be more pronounced there. I guess this is because young girls are typically more advanced linguistically, socially and emotionally than boys of the same age. Of course this isn't always the case but *typically* it is.

So, while the girls are being told: 'clever girl', 'good girl', 'what a beautiful picture', the boys are being told:

> 'John – if only you could sit still for a minute and listen then you'd do much better.'

> 'Paul – if you put as much effort into your work as you do into messing about then you could really achieve.'

> 'Ringo – as for you, young man, you need to focus more! I'm fed up of repeating myself for your sake.'

Notice what the boys are being told – if you concentrate more, try harder, listen better, then you will do better. These are *growth mindset* messages. It is a pity they come in the form of criticism but, nonetheless, they are *growth* messages.

Girls, on the other hand, are being praised into developing a fixed mindset through terms such as clever, bright, good, and so on.

Of course these are generalisations. There are many girls with a *growth mindset* and many boys with a *fixed mindset*; the point is that children develop a particular mindset due in part to the praise and encouragement they receive.

So, if we want children to develop a growth mindset, and that would seem the best choice if we want children to be learners, then we need to think about what and how we praise.

> Confusion is a common occurrence in maths and science, where, unlike most verbal areas, new material often involves completely new skills, concepts, or conceptual systems. So we created a new task for students to learn and for half of the students we placed some confusing material near the beginning.
>
> What we found was that bright girls didn't cope at all well with this confusion. In fact, the higher the girl's IQ, the worse she did. Many high IQ

girls were unable to learn the material after experiencing confusion. This didn't happen to boys. For them, the higher their IQ, the better they learned. The confusion only energized them. Since our high IQ girls had done wonderfully well when they didn't bump up against difficulty, what we're looking at here isn't a difference in ability, but a difference in how students cope with experiences that may call their ability into question – whether they feel challenged by them or demoralized by them.

(Dweck, 2006)[25]

Comparing test scores

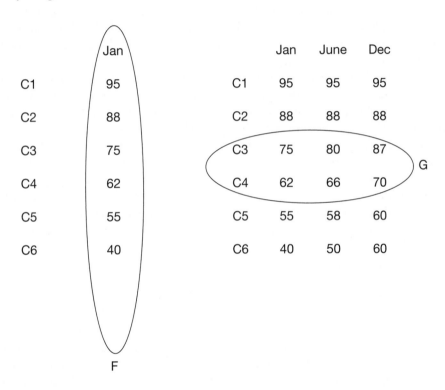

	Jan
C1	95
C2	88
C3	75
C4	62
C5	55
C6	40

F

	Jan	June	Dec
C1	95	95	95
C2	88	88	88
C3	75	80	87
C4	62	66	70
C5	55	58	60
C6	40	50	60

G

Is my child top of the class?

Many parents are obsessed with finding out if their child is cleverer than everyone else's. When I was a teacher, I rarely had a conversation with a parent without them asking, directly or indirectly, whether their child was top, middle or bottom of the pack.

I understand the motivation to find out and I am certainly not immune to the same desire to know. However, this really shouldn't matter for a number of reasons:

(a) Learning is about making progress, not about being better or worse than someone else.

(b) Comparisons more often than not lead to despondency, worry or complacency.

(c) Children will be in a certain group only for a short time. Once they move, the comparisons will be obsolete. What will remain is their attitude to learning itself.

The illustrations on p. 43 make this point. They show the scores achieved by six children: Child 1 (C1) to Child 6 (C6).

In the first diagram, someone with a fixed (F) mindset is comparing data vertically. They're hoping their child is C1 or C2, or at the very least C3 or C4. They'll certainly be worried if their child is C5 or C6. And yet this set of figures tells us *nothing* about learning.

By comparison, the second diagram shows the first set of scores together with the subsequent scores achieved by each student. Now at last there is some information about learning. We can see quite clearly which children are making progress (C3, C4 and C6 in particular) and which are not (C1 and C2).

So, if I'm a parent with a fixed mindset (F), then I might be quite happy, maybe even boastful, that my child is C1 or C2. However, if I'm a parent of C1 or C2 and I have a growth mindset (G), then I would be concerned as to why my child is not making any progress at all. Are they not being challenged? Is the work too easy? Are they being allowed to coast? Or has the scoring system reached its limit? Whichever of these it might be, I'd want to help bring about some changes.

You get what you measure

I had the great pleasure of listening to Nick Zeniuk presenting at a conference in Malaysia some years ago. Together with Peter Senge and the late W. Edwards Deming, Zeniuk was responsible for building the 1995–8 Lincoln Continental, a car that set company performance records in terms of quality, timing and cost savings. A key to their success was realising that 'you get what you measure'. Instead of checking time worked, they began to measure the level of collaboration between colleagues and almost immediately changed the culture of the company for the better.

I believe it is the same with children.

If we focus on correct answers, then that is what children will infer is important. This can lead to them doing whatever is needed to get full marks – including choosing the easy option, because that increases the chance of getting everything right, or even cheating.

Whereas, if we clearly show that we are impressed with effort, determination, desire and concentration, this then can lead to children being more willing to undertake harder challenges and to set themselves more complex tasks – in other words, to engage in learning behaviour.

So the next time a child gets ten out of ten in a test, I'd recommend going for one of the following responses:

- 'Wow, that's a good score – did you find you had to work hard to get everything right?'
- 'Congratulations – that must have required a lot of concentration to get full marks.'
- 'Well done – you got ten out of ten for right answers. So what score would you give yourself for effort required?'
- 'That's a better score than you got on the last test you took. What do you think made the difference?'

Note to teachers – Praise and feedback should be kept separate.

There are some interesting notes on p. 121 of John Hattie's *Visible Learning for Teachers* (2012), in which he states:

> Praise includes little information about performance on the task and praise provides little help in answering the three feedback questions (where am I going; how am I doing; where should I go next?). . . . Hyland and Hyland (2006) noted that almost half of teachers' feedback was praise, and that premature and gratuitous praise confused students and discouraged revisions. . . . The message is . . . praise the students and make them feel welcomed to your class and worthwhile as learners, but if you wish to make a major difference to learning, leave praise out of feedback about learning.

A cautionary note about effort

It is easy to get carried away with the idea that effort is all that matters. That is simply not true. Even if I put huge effort into practising something – but that something is irrelevant to the desired outcome (e.g. spending hours rehearsing the wrong lines for a play) – then success is unlikely.

Success comes from trying hard at the right thing, at the right time, with the right support from the right people and using talents wisely (and perhaps hoping for a bit of luck along the way).

At the end of this chapter, I share a story about my daughter and the varying levels of effort she puts in to swimming and dancing. Happily she is making wonderful progress in her swimming. This is *partly* as a result of her efforts but it is also because of expert teaching that focuses on technique, challenge and enjoyment.

Genetics also play a role, dare I say it. She swims with a friend of hers who is built like a whippet – there is not an ounce of fat on him. When he swims, a part of his effort has to go into not sinking, whereas Ava doesn't have that problem – she floats pretty well!

The key to developing a growth mindset is to focus on progress. Talk about progress, praise progress, celebrate it and, above all, recognise it as synonymous with learning. Progress is learning and learning is progress.

Setting tests that challenge

I used to loathe the spelling tests I was obliged to give as a teacher because the results never seemed to vary. A handful of children always got ten out of ten, the majority typically got eight out of ten and a few children would get only three or four out of ten. The children who got top marks seemed to do so with consummate ease, leaving me to worry they might believe success always comes easily. Those with middling marks seemed to be frustrated by never achieving a perfect score, sometimes resulting in a drop in motivation. As for those who always scored poorly, these tests seemed to confirm what they already suspected: that they were stupid. (How can it be legal in any country in the world that children go to school and end up learning that they are stupid?)

These spelling tests set performance targets: every child in the same class was supposed to achieve the same level with the same words.

To get around this problem, I used to give a pre-test first. This involved reading out between fifteen and twenty words for children to spell. Each child would then mark their neighbour's paper as I revealed the correct spellings. Once the results were returned to the rightful owner, I asked each child to pick ten words from their pre-test paper that they'd got wrong. This list then became their very own learning goal for the following week.

Incidentally, if some children had less than ten wrong answers on their pre-test then I'd give them an additional list of more complex words to choose from. And if I suspected some students were intentionally getting answers wrong so as to avoid the more challenging words, I'd offer them some really easy words until they realised progress was the key – not boasting about the highest score.

Growth mindset and school grades

An issue that arises time and again when I'm working with teachers on developing growth mindsets is the problem of assessment and grades. They tell me parents demand grades, pupils expect them and governments compile them. Yet grades often run in opposition to learning, particularly when viewed as an end in themselves.

In a fixed-mindset world, grades measure how clever pupils are in comparison with each other. Similarly, league tables identify the best schools as well as the schools to avoid.

However, in a growth-mindset world, grades give an indication about progress towards learning goals. They also offer evidence to help decide whether learning strategies need to be adapted or not.

So if you work in a school (or business) or your child attends a school that you would like to see developing growth mindsets, here are some suggestions:

1   Make assessment criteria clear

Receiving a percentage or grade for a piece of work gives the impression of precision. However, if it does not match clear criteria then it will give no idea as to what has been mastered or what could be improved. Instead, clear learning intentions, success criteria and the sharing of exemplar work will help children (and their parents) to understand what is expected and how their work will be judged.

Furthermore, a clear idea of what is needed to achieve a particular grade will help enormously. Many institutions simply state that 70 per cent is needed for an 'A' grade; 60 per cent for a 'B' and so on. Whereas it would be much more useful if they also identified the criteria that would need to be met to achieve 70 per cent – in other words to show exactly what an 'A' grade piece of work looks like, what a 'B' grade would look like and so on.

2   Don't grade every piece of work

Some teachers worry that students won't complete a task that doesn't count towards their overall grade. However, growth mindsets can be encouraged when some assignments are set that will not be graded – thus creating a safe space to make mistakes – or have alternative criteria for evaluation based on effort, creativity, persistence and teamwork, which are made clear to the students.

3   Comments before grades

Written feedback that prompts a proactive response from the learner is far more effective at improving performance than grades are. However, a number of studies[26] have shown that most pupils ignore written feedback if it is accompanied by a grade. They seem to believe that the grade is king! If they get a good grade there's nothing more to be learned from reading the comments and if they get a poor grade then why rub salt in the wound? So try to give comments first and then grades at a later date, or alternate your feedback on assignments between comments only and grades only.

4   Assess as you go

If I was going to build a wall, I wouldn't dream of finishing the job before checking levels and angles; I'd keep checking and adjusting as I go. And yet, so often, children (and adults) are expected to complete an assignment before their teacher (or line manager) assesses their work. How bizarre! Assessment should be part of the learning process. For example, randomly select a piece of unfinished work and display it for everyone to suggest ways to improve. Or, engage individuals in reviewing their work mid-assignment. Both procedures will help enormously to improve everyone's learning. Incidentally, 'assess' comes from the Latin, *cassimere*, which means 'to sit beside'.

5   Grade progress

Where possible, identify a starting point so that progress can be identified and remarked upon. The alternative spelling test I mentioned on p. 46 is a good example of this. Progress is more likely when learning goals, rather than performance goals (see p. 13), are identified and worked towards.

6   Use growth mindset language

Use every opportunity to model, articulate and teach a growth mindset. Treat and talk about tests as data that will help make decisions about where next; praise pupils for strategies and improvements rather than perfect performances; base lessons on progress ('let's see how much progress we've made so far and where we could go next'); and focus on learning goals rather than performance goals (see p. 13).

7   Grow assessment-capable learners

After examining 60,000 research studies in education, Hattie found that the most effective way to improve learning is to help pupils become assessment-capable. The effect size is as high as 1.44 – the equivalent of three times the normal rate of progress (see p. 26 for an explanation of effect size).

So if you can help children understand where they are in their learning, how they got there and what they need to do next, you are likely to have a powerfully positive impact on their chances of success. Questions such as 'what helped you achieve that?'; 'what would you do differently if you were to do it all over again?'; 'what can you do now that you couldn't do before and how do you feel about that?' are all likely to help.

Another cautionary note

Having a fixed mindset and achieving good exam grades are *not* incompatible. Many thousands of students each year graduate from school with excellent grades, despite having a fixed mindset. Similarly, those with a growth mindset aren't necessarily the people most likely to achieve the best grades. So why then should we favour a growth mindset?

The answer lies in what people of a different mindset do when things go wrong. All too often school poses little challenge for some students – they are able to hit school-set or government-set performance targets easily. And when this happens again and again, those students begin to believe that (a) they are gifted and (b) they do not need to try.

By contrast, some students really work hard to achieve good grades and frequently set themselves learning goals as opposed to performance goals (i.e. goals that stretch and challenge rather than goals that simply get them over the finishing line). These are the students most likely to possess a growth mindset.

Now fast-forward to university or work and imagine that both sets of students are facing challenges that are initially too difficult for them. The chances are that those with a fixed mindset will wilt under the pressure, give up or doubt their own abilities; whereas those with a growth mindset will probably rise to the challenge, seek advice and support or try to find alternative routes to solve the problems.

PRAISE QUIZ 1

Based on what you know from reading this chapter, which of these stickers encourage a growth mindset and which might support a fixed mindset? Answers on p. 50.

FIGURE 3.4 Reward stickers

PRAISE QUIZ 2

Which of these phrases would help develop a growth mindset?

1 Good girl
2 Great effort
3 Clever boy
4 Perfect
5 You're #1
6 It's everything I hoped for
7 Inspired
8 What a talent
9 What a genius
10 You figured it out.
11 Keep up the good work
12 A+
13 Great discovery
14 You're improving
15 Ten out of ten
16 Bright group
17 I admire your determination
18 Such a talented artist
19 What a great idea
20 Wonderful progress.

QUIZ ANSWERS

Stickers

The stickers more likely to encourage a growth mindset than the others: *Engaged Learner, Top Progress; I'm Star of the Week for my determination and effort; Ask me what brilliant things I'm trying.*

Praise phrases

Though praise depends on context, tone of voice, relationship between the people involved and so on, here are the most likely answers:

–   Growth mindset encouraged by praise phrases 2, 7, 10, 13, 14, 17, 19 and 20.

–   Fixed mindset encouraged by 1, 3, 4, 5, 9, 16 and 18.

–   More questionable ones include:

   6 – This sets the speaker up as judge and jury. A much more positive phrase would be: 'I bet your success makes you feel good.' This teaches children to be intrinsically motivated rather than rely on affirmations from others.

   8 and 12 – Depends whether these are being used to describe an action (in which case, it's growth praise) or a person (in which case, it could be fixed praise).

   11 and 15 – Depends whether the good work has been easy to achieve (fixed praise) or a challenge (growth praise).

A final story about praise

I'd like to finish this chapter with a story about my daughter because, bless her, she's been my unwitting guinea pig during my transition from fixed to growth mindset.

For the first thirty-something years of my life, I had a fixed mindset. I believed intelligence was hereditary, that there were some things I was good at and other things I'd never be able to do, and that was that. Then I heard my good friend, Barry Hymer, speaking about Dweck's work and this really got me thinking. Spurred on by wanting to put things right generally – but also specifically for the sake of my daughter who was now eighteen months old – I began reading as many research papers and books by Carol Dweck as I could.

Unfortunately, the first thing I did was to stop praising my daughter! I was so worried about the effect my fixed mindset praise might have on her (clever girl, you're brilliant, my perfect princess, and so on) that I thought it would be better to say nothing rather than risk saying something wrong. How's that for a fixed mindset – play it safe rather than take a risk!

Then I spotted an opportunity to try out some new ways to praise: Ava was about to start swimming lessons. I've always been good at swimming* and so it seemed like a good context to begin with.

Anyway, back to my daughter and her swimming. By the time she was two years old, she had started swimming lessons *and* dancing lessons. Though she enjoyed both, she definitely preferred the dancing and dreamt of one day becoming a professional ballerina.

NB. Please note that I tell the following story with the full blessing of my daughter's Grandma (my mother-in-law). We get on very well and she knows I tell the story simply to illustrate a point rather than to mock her in any way.

As I write this, Ava is almost six years old and excels at swimming. However, she has started and stopped dancing lessons more times than I care to remember. This is partly a reflection of the high quality guidance from her swimming teachers, compared with the standard of instruction in her first ballet and jazz classes, but I'm convinced it is also down to the type of praise she has received for each.

More often than not, I am the one to take Ava swimming. When she does well, I explain this is because of her effort, determination and willingness to listen and try. When she doesn't do well, I tell her that learning often involves taking two steps forward and one back, or I point out that she didn't concentrate/try as hard as she had the week before (I only say this last bit if it is true!). I avoid telling her she's a brilliant swimmer so that when she doesn't do so well one week, she won't then begin to think that she is all of a sudden a bad swimmer.

As for her dancing, Grandma used to take her. My mother-in-law, who breaks into my house without an invitation, tells her granddaughter: 'Wow, Ava – you're the best ballerina in the world.'

Initially my daughter loved hearing such praise from Grandma and beamed with pride. However, her motivation soon started to drop when she realised that Grandma would lavish praise upon her whether she had tried or not. Though this might sound great – praised if you do, praised if you don't – it undermined the effectiveness of the praise. When Ava larked about during her lesson and still had praise lavished on her, she felt guilty as if she were lying to Grandma by not owning up to her lack of endeavour. And when she worked her little tutu off but received the same praise she'd heard the week before, she felt short-changed! Eventually she asked me why she had to go dancing with Grandma. I replied: 'We all have our crosses to bear, darling.'

What this story shows is that praise can be far more effective if we refer to children's *actions* (their dancing and swimming), rather than to the child as a dancer or swimmer.

---

* I say 'always been good at swimming' in a tongue-in-cheek manner because that's what I would've said once upon a time. Now I know I'm good at it because of the hundreds of hours I spent swimming at primary school, the dozens of competitions I entered while at secondary school and the year I spent training to be a swimming coach and lifeguard instructor in the United States in the early 1990s!

For example:

Avoid labels such as	Praise actions such as
■ Great swimmer	■ Great swimming
■ Wonderful writer	■ Wonderful writing
■ Elegant dancer	■ Elegant dancing
■ Superb thinker	■ Superb thinking
■ Genius.	■ Admirable effort.

Top tips for praise

1   Use praise that leads to a growth mindset

To give ourselves, and therefore the children we come into contact with, the best chance of developing (or maintaining) a growth mindset, we would do well to use language and phrases such as:

- If you have to try, you must be learning.
- Challenge is good for us.
- Dedication's what you need (good old Roy Castle).
- Great effort!
- You succeeded because you worked hard, got help when you needed it and kept going to the end.
- I've not been able to play the piano – yet! (not: I'm hopeless at the piano).

2   Draw attention to top performers

Explain the success of people such as Usain Bolt and Martha Lane Fox in terms of it being as much to do with their dedication, determination, focus and passion, as it is to do with genetics or being in the place at the right time.

As Carol Dweck said at conferences where we both gave presentations in June 2010: 'Genetics is just the starting point.'[27]

3   Praise the action, not the child

Praise children for something they have control over (effort, focus, determination and so on). This will empower them to learn and grow.

For example:
Great running, reading, writing, effort, determination, problem solving!
not:
Great runner, brilliant reader/writer, clever child, you are a natural problem solver!

4 Make praise credible

Don't tell a child they are a great reader when they are not. Not only might the child reject this as pity praise but other children who hear might begin to question the sincerity of your praise. Instead, praise children for effort and progress.

For example: Great reading – you're making fantastic progress!

not:
You're the best reader ever!

5 Compare progress rather than children

Praise a child in comparison to themselves, not to others.

For example:
Your swimming is so much better than last week (because you're concentrating more than you were last time).

not:
You're a much better swimmer than that child over there!

Further reading

For further information about praise, mindsets and issues about talents and genetics, I recommend the following:

Books

Mindset by Carol Dweck (ISBN: 978–0345472328)
Bounce by Matthew Syed (ISBN: 978–0007350520)
Talent is Overrated by Geoff Colvin (ISBN: 978–1857885194)

Online

www.brainology.us
www.carol-dweck.co.uk

For schools

Challenging Learning by James Nottingham (ISBN: 978–0956482808)
Gifted and Talented Pocketbook by Barry Hymer (ISBN: 978–1906610012)
New Kinds of Smart: How the science of learnable intelligence is changing education by Guy Claxton and Bill Lucas (ISBN: 978–0335236183

4

Learning to think for themselves

The development of general ability for independent thinking and judgment should always be placed foremost, not the acquisition of special knowledge.
(Albert Einstein, 1950)[28]

FIGURE 4.1 Albert Einstein, 1879–1955

Introduction

As I watch my young son grow, I am fascinated to see how he learns to think. After just a few months, he seemed to deliberately compare one object with another by studying each one in turn through sight, sound or, more often, taste. By the time he was eleven months old, he was thinking of alternative ways to give food to our dog, Hector. We'd tell him not to give his finger-food to the dog, so he'd smile at us, put the food behind his back and waggle it for the dog to take. Now he is two, he has begun to reason with us: 'Not go to my bed, go to Mummy/Daddy's bed. I go to my bed, I'll cry'.

This was an almost nightly argument for a week or two. My son's natural development of thinking provokes a question: since he has already learnt how to think, does he really need to be taught how to do it more?

To answer this, it is important to distinguish between types of thinking which, to my mind, consist of two main categories: routine and reflective.

Routine thinking, including the thinking we do almost subconsciously when, for example, riding a bike, walking or quoting our telephone number.

Reflective thinking, including thinking about the consequences of our actions and deciding on the relative importance of factors affecting our decisions about what to think or do.

If my son learns to speak or write fluently but then does so thoughtlessly or inconsiderately, he is likely to upset himself and others. If he memorises lots of facts but doesn't learn how to use them wisely, then his knowledge will be limited in its application. I want him, therefore, to have the opportunity at home and at school to improve, among other things, the proficient, reflective and sociable aspects of his thinking.

Why do we need more thinking?

1   Thinking is needed for a healthy society

All too often individuals, families, organisations and communities live with the consequences of poorly thought out decisions, biased judgements, unreasonable behaviour, narrow or limited perspectives and unexamined values.

Yet if people learned to be more thoughtful, by asking better questions, articulating problems, engaging in respectful dialogue with each other and thinking collaboratively, then many of these problems could be avoided. Prejudice, or pre-judging, would reduce; knee-jerk reactions would diminish; and thoughtless actions would be restricted.

Of course, some of those in power might prefer citizens not to think (or, at least, to be obedient) and I certainly don't want to suggest that an unreflective life is necessarily a bad thing. Many unquestioned traditions bring joy to people's lives and many actions are enjoyable precisely because they appear to be spontaneous. But perhaps we only know these enjoyable actions are harmless because we've thought about them before.

2 Learning how to learn is the key to lifelong learning

Lifelong learning depends upon learning *how* to learn and being willing to learn. Without these attributes, children cannot become independent or adaptable learners.

Learning how to learn requires that children ask questions, give reasons, organise information and understand concepts, all of which are skills of thinking. Children also need to be able to generalise, find exceptions, challenge assumptions, paraphrase and predict. And since our world is changing more rapidly than at any time in history, it seems that the ability to learn, adapt and use judgement will be of the utmost importance.

3 Thinking enhances reading and writing

Galina Dolya points out in her excellent book, *The Key to Learning*, that the best way to help young children prepare for school is not to push them into learning their letters and numbers; instead, she argues, it is better to help them learn how to think about and decode a wide range of child-friendly symbols such as pictures, maps, plans and models so that they are 'ready and have the ability to learn' by the time they get to school.[29]

4 Thinking will be tested in exams

Recently I looked through every exam paper for eleven- and fourteen-year-olds in England and all the GCSE exams sat by sixteen-year-olds in 2008. It was interesting to see that almost all the papers began with questions that required straightforward factual answers, attracting just a point or two. However, subsequent questions were more extended and required pupils to use thinking skills such as reasoning, explaining, comparing and contrasting. These later questions attracted most marks.[30]

For example, take a look at the exam question on p. 58. This is from OCR's GCSE History (Modern World) Paper 1, sat by many sixteen-year-olds in June 2008.

Consider the thinking skills that are needed to answer this question. Even with extensive knowledge of the Depression, how could pupils answer this question fully, bearing in mind it is worth 7 marks (10 per cent of the whole paper), unless they have been taught how to reason and to understand the arguments and counter-arguments necessary for 'proving' a case one way or another?

Also shown is a typical task from a science paper for eleven-year-olds.

Does this photograph prove that Hoover's policies did little to help people during the Depression? (*7 marks*)

FIGURE 4.2 Photo accompanying exam question

Jamal says: 'I think if you put the ice cubes inside lots of plastic bags they will stay frozen for longer.'

What sort of statement has Jamal made: an observation, a prediction, a conclusion or a measurement? Explain your answer. *(3 marks)*

Thinking skills tested in exams

On the next page is a list of the main thinking skills tested by national exams in the UK and in Australia. My work in these two countries has led me to research their exam papers but, from my work elsewhere, I understand that a very similar list could be drawn from exams in other countries:

ANALYSE	ESTIMATE	REPRESENT
ANTICIPATE	EVALUATE	RESPOND
APPLY	EXEMPLIFY	SEQUENCE
CAUSAL-LINK	EXPLORE	SIMPLIFY
CHOOSE	GENERALISE	SHOW HOW
CLASSIFY	GIVE EXAMPLES	SOLVE
COMPARE	GIVE REASONS	SORT
CONCLUDE	GROUP	SUMMARISE
CONNECT	HYPOTHESISE	SUPPORT
CONTRAST	IDENTIFY	TEST
DECIDE	INFER	VERIFY
DEFINE	PREDICT	VISUALISE
DESCRIBE	QUESTION	
ELABORATE	RANK	

Flexible, insightful and productive thinking

What is 'good' thinking? Does it mean being more efficient, ethical or wise? Or is it more to do with innovation, critique and collaboration?

After studying the work of leading thinkers, I propose that good thinking is flexible, insightful and productive.

This, I believe, captures the essence of proposals by (among others) Edward de Bono, Art Costa, David Perkins, Guy Claxton, Lane Clark and Matthew Lipman. There is limited use for productive thinking if it is not flexible, nor for insights if they are unproductive. Thus, good thinking is a combination of all three of these.

Exploring this further, I recommend you focus children's energies initially on developing the skills listed below and on pp. 9–10.

Following the list, there is a selection of games and activities that will help children put into practice at least one of the skills marked with an asterisk. Obviously, playing each game just once will not result in children perfecting the associated skill, but it is a start!

Thinking activities with children

In the games that follow, please note:

(a) I've highlighted the main thinking skills involved but other skills will typically be developed as well.

(b) Although there is no right or wrong answer, there are probably better ones in each case. To help identify the higher quality responses, encourage children to give reasons and to compare the relative merits of each answer they come up with.

Process information

- Find relevant information
- Compare and contrast *
- Sort, classify and sequence *
- Make connections *
- Identify problems.

Reasoning

- Give reasons *
- Infer and deduce *
- Apply logic
- Present balanced arguments
- Identify flaws in others' arguments.

Inquire

- Ask relevant questions *
- Predict outcomes
- Seek further details *
- Push for clarity and precision
- Use precise language. *

Creativity

- Look for alternatives and possibilities
- Generate hypotheses
- Search for value *
- Think flexibly
- Ask 'What if? *

Evaluate

- Develop criteria
- Check accuracy *
- Identify improvements *
- Test relevance and significance
- Benchmark.

1 Odd One Out

Main skills involved: Comparing and contrasting.

Aim: Take three objects and ask children to decide which is the odd one out and why. There should be many answers.

Example answers (all answers valid)

Drum – the only one that is: positioned straight in the picture; played with drumsticks; is a percussion instrument.

Saxophone – the only one that: is blown to play; is made of brass; has a reed; has a tube; easily disassembles.

Guitar – the only one that: has strings; is often played with a plectrum; has a neck; comes as one piece.

For older children, you could select a range of concepts for comparison. For example:

- Happiness – Contentment – Enjoyment
- Decision – Fact – Evidence
- Sport – War – Games
- Media – Story – Books
- Loan – Earnings – Credit.

More examples also on: www.bbc.co.uk/cbeebies.

FIGURE 4.3 Instruments to compare and contrast

2 That Is Exactly What I Was Thinking

Main skills involved: Making connections.

Aim: Child A says what they were thinking of. Child B says what they were thinking of. Child A should then try to make enough links to suggest that they were both in fact thinking of the same thing.

Example: Child A says 'Rhinoceros'; Child B says 'Tulip'. Child A then says: 'That's exactly what I was thinking because my rhino is in a Dutch zoo and lives in a field surrounded by tulips.'
Variations

- Child A says his/her word in French (or another foreign language) and Child B gives his/her word in English.

- Child A thinks of something living while Child B thinks of something inanimate.

- Child A thinks of something abstract, Child B of something concrete.

FIGURE 4.4 A very special rhino

3 Diamond Ranking

Main skills involved: Sorting, classifying and sequencing.

Example: Start with the animals below. If the children are young (two- to six-year-olds), ask them to pick three animals they think they'd see at Christmas time (reindeer, cat, horse perhaps?) or that would make the best pets (cat, rabbit, tortoise?). Once they are used to selecting and ranking them, increase the challenge until they are ready for the older children's activity described on p. 64.

For older children, ask them to put the animals in order of cuteness (they could use the *diamond rank* pattern shown opposite with a top spot, two second equals, three third equals and so on. Or, they could go for a straight line, pyramid or similar.

Once they have completed the first rank, ask them to choose their own criteria (e.g. probability of seeing them in a house; the population size in the world/your country; the length of their hair).

Other things to rank: Objects; food; routes to a destination; games; professions. (Many adults struggle with this last one because they feel it is unethical to rank people, but it could be done by percentage of women in the job; starting salary; distance travelled in a day; and so on.)

FIGURE 4.5 Ranking animals

4 Inference Squares

Main skills involved: Inferring, deducing and asking relevant questions.

Aim: Distinguish between what we know for certain, what we can infer and what questions we could ask when reading a news article, picture book or similar source of information.

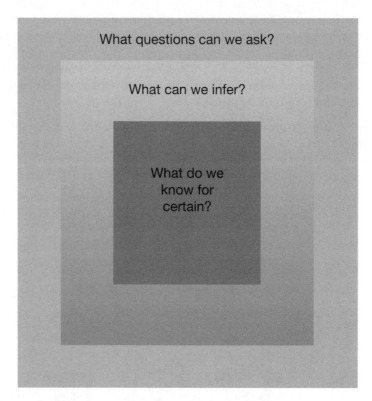

FIGURE 4.6 Inference squares

5 The Three Whys (Men)

Main skills involved: Giving reasons.

Background: Over the years, I've noticed a common barrier to developing thinking skills: children (and adults) are rarely asked for reasons to support their opinions. It seems to me that – so long as a child can express himself/herself articulately – then they are praised for this, even if they are merely repeating something they've heard rather than expressing a well thought-out idea.

For a person to present a reasoned argument they must:

■ give an opinion (their conclusion);

■ intend the argument to be persuasive.

Listen to those around you – how often do they express opinions without offering reasons?

To begin changing this habit, try *The Three Whys* (because this will help children get used to the idea that there can be many reasons for an opinion or action).

Aim: When a child gives an opinion, ask why they think that. After they've given their reason, again ask why. Then after they've given their second reason, ask why for a third time.

For example, on my website, challenginglearning.com/resources, there is a video clip called *P4C with Nursery Children* in which I'm leading a discussion with three-year-old children (see Chapter 7 for more about what I'm trying to achieve in this session).

In the clip you can observe me asking Ava (the girl on the far right of the circle) three whys. The dialogue goes along the lines of:

Me: If I put this builder's hat on your head then you become Bob the Builder; but if I put this name badge that belongs to Daniel next to you, do you become 'Daniel'?

Ava: No.

Me: Why not? (*first why*)

Ava: Because it's silly.

Me: Why is it silly? (*second why*)

Ava: Because it feels funny.

Me: Why does it feel funny? (*third why*)

Ava: Because my name is Ava. I don't want to be called Daniel because that's not my real name.

Notice how Ava's answers are developing as a result of each why. This may not have happened if I hadn't asked so many 'whys'.

Of course, this doesn't always work. Many children might shrug their shoulders or simply say: 'Just cos', but over time they will develop their reasoning skills.

An example of older children giving reasons without being asked can be viewed in a short video (*Granny or Goldfish?*) available on p4c.com and YouTube.

6 Copy Charts

Main skills involved: Seeking further details.

Aim: The object of the game is to reproduce a picture, graph or map (e.g. the one above) with as much detail and accuracy as possible. To make things more challenging, this should be done from memory. This works best with groups of children, but can be played by individuals.

For example, with groups of children, the first child would look at the diagram for 20 seconds. They would then return to their group and describe what they've seen while beginning to reproduce a copy onto a blank sheet of paper. Meanwhile, the second child would get to look at the original for 20 seconds, return to the group and assist with the reproduction.

Once all the children in each group have had their turn at viewing the diagram, it is a good idea to give the groups a chance to talk. Suggest they think about possible strategies they might employ to improve their chances of success in the next round. Then once again, give each child a chance to look at the diagram and to return to their group with further details to add to their replica.

Other objects to copy: This can be played with almost any relevant object, picture or even sound. The key to it is for children to recreate accurate details from memory, using any thinking skill that might help.

FIGURE 4.7 Treasure island map

7 Say What You Mean

Main skills involved: Using precise language.

Background: My first book, *Challenging Learning*,[31] is being translated into various languages, including Norwegian. This is helping me to realise just how complex translating is, particularly when English has so many more words than, for example, Norwegian. I'm reliably informed this is because English has more varied roots (including Latin, ancient Greek, Old French and Norse) than other languages. This breadth of vocabulary lends itself nicely to this next game.

Aim: Ask children to identify similarities and differences of meaning between words that are related. For example:

> Probably – Possibly – Potentially – Presumably
>
> Original – Artistic – Unique – Innovative
>
> Animal – Beast – Pet – Creature
>
> Love – Lust – Like – Desire
>
> Worship – Honour – Praise – Idolise
>
> Sport – Game – Competition – Pastime.

Other examples: The comparisons do not have to be of words with related meanings; a comparison of when to use 'why', 'when', 'who' and so on is also useful.

8 Opposites Attract

Main skills involved: Searching for value.

Background: In his books, Edward de Bono writes about 'Provocative Operations'.[32] This is a strategy for creating new ideas, however illogical, then looking for their value.

For example: If I want to come up with a business plan for a new restaurant, de Bono advocates using a provocative operation to consider opening a restaurant that does the exact opposite of what you'd expect – for instance, *not* serving food. This might include:

(a) welcoming customers who bring their own food;

(b) combining a culinary school with a restaurant so that customers learn to cook the food that they're about to eat;

(c) opening a restaurant that only served diet milkshakes.

Then from these ideas, identify the possibilities that could be included within your actual business plan. For example, opening a restaurant that had *Masterchef* evenings; that allowed customers to bring their own herbs and spices; or one that catered for dieters by listing the calorie-ratings for each dish.

Aim: Think of the ways to achieve the following then identify the value from your ideas that could then be applied to achieving the opposite:

- receiving as many complaints as possible;
- learning how to ride a bicycle without ever getting on a bike;
- appreciating art without looking at it;
- exercising a dog without talking him for a walk.

9 What If

Main skills involved: Asking 'What if?'

Background: In his wonderful book *Would You Rather?*, John Burningham gives children choices such as: 'Would you rather be made to eat spider stew, slug dumplings, mashed worms or drink snail squash?'[33]

A favourite alternative to this is 'What if?'

For example:

'What if you had wings, what would you do?'

or

'What if our politicians were chosen in an X Factor-style competition?'

Here are some to try with children,

What if . . .

- . . . dogs were as big as horses and horses were as small as guinea pigs?
- . . . books were banned in school?
- . . . cars were outlawed?
- . . . you could choose which days would have 20 hours in them and which would have 28 hours?
- . . . people were paid less the older they got?
- . . . everyone had to move house once every 3 years?
- . . . parents set schoolwork instead of teachers?
- . . . rats did the work of bees?
- . . . cows produced wine rather than milk?
- . . . everyone in the world had to learn esperanto?
- . . . technology stopped developing?

---

10 Venn diagrams

Main skills involved: Checking for accuracy.

Venn diagrams: Hated by children in maths lessons but great as a visual tool for thinking! They are also a good way to clarify ideas and give accurate descriptions.

For example: The following Venn diagram would illustrate accurately the difference between pets and farm animals.

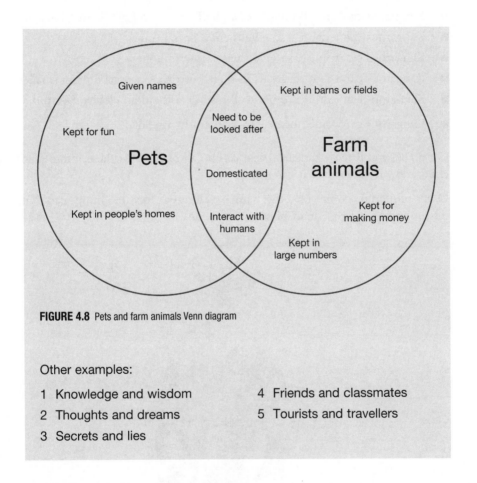

FIGURE 4.8 Pets and farm animals Venn diagram

Other examples:

1 Knowledge and wisdom
2 Thoughts and dreams
3 Secrets and lies
4 Friends and classmates
5 Tourists and travellers

Suggestions for other comparisons: Heroes and villains; shape and size; talking and communicating; music and noise; sport and war; children and adults; rain and snow; school and work.

11 Kangaroos Can't

Main skills involved: Identifying improvements.

Aim: To create animals or objects that children think will be suited to a greater number of environments or activities.

For example: Begin by thinking of a kangaroo. Identify what it can do, then think of how it could be adapted to do what it can't do normally.

- Kangaroos can't fly – so give them wings.
- Kangaroos can't reach the leaves a giraffe can – so give them a long neck.
- Kangaroos can't swim – so give them a dorsal fin.
- Kangaroos can't sing – so give them a microphone.
- Kangaroos can't join meerkats in their burrows – so make them smaller.
- Kangaroos can't drink from a well – so give them an elephant's trunk.
- Kangaroos can't ride horses – so sit them in a saddle.

On p. 70, you'll see a kangaroo that can do all but one of these things (can your children spot which one it can't do?).

Older children could use the same technique for designing cars, musical instruments, the latest smart phone, and so on.

JNP

FIGURE 4.9 A very talented kangaroo

Top tips for thinking

1   Develop routine and reflective thinking

Routine thinking is what we do subconsciously when completing tasks that are easy for us, whereas reflective thinking includes considering the consequences of our actions and what is most effective, efficient or ethical. Good thinking requires high levels of both.

2   Good thinking is flexible, insightful and productive

Productive thinking is limited if it is not flexible and insights are limited if they are unproductive. Good thinking, then, requires a combination of all three. The activities on pp. 61–70 will help towards developing good thinking.

3   Thinking will be tested in exams

Though most exam papers begin with straightforward factual answers, these only attract a few marks each. The questions that account for the most significant portion of the final grade require children to be able to think reflectively. The main skills tested include giving reasons, sorting and classifying, making connections, predicting outcomes, searching for value and checking accuracy. So the assertion by many commentators that children simply need more knowledge is limited, misguided and, ironically, factually incorrect.

Children need to develop their thinking skills as much as they need to learn facts.

Further reading

There are many excellent books about thinking. Here are a few of my favourites.

Books

Critical Thinking for Students by Roy van den Brink-Budgen
(ISBN: 978–1845283865)

De Bono's Thinking Course by Edward de Bono (ISBN: 978–0563370734)

New Kinds of Smart by Bill Lucas and Guy Claxton (ISBN: 978–0335236183)

Radical Encouragement by Steve Williams and Rupert Wegerif
(ISBN: 978–1904806035)

Thinking Skills and Early Childhood Education by Patrick Costello
(ISBN: 978–1853465512)

Twenty Thinking Tools by Philip Cam (ISBN: 978–0864315014)

> If you make people think they're thinking, they'll love you; but if you really make them think they'll hate you.
>
> Don Marquis (American humourist, journalist and author)

5

Helping children to be wise

> Before you become too entranced with gorgeous gadgets and mesmerizing video displays, let me remind you that information is not knowledge, knowledge is not wisdom, and wisdom is not foresight. Each grows out of the other, and we need them all.
>
> (Arthur C. Clarke, 1917–2008)

Thinking wisely

In 2003, I attended an international conference on Philosophy for Children in Bulgaria. In addition to the 200 delegates from around the world, the organisers also invited some local teenagers to take part in proceedings. Midway through the four-day event, I was asked to facilitate a community of inquiry with these teenagers for the other delegates to observe.

I began the session with a fictional story about two hunters, Hank and Frank, who are chased by a talking bear. The teenagers then created a number of philosophical questions from which they chose their favourite: 'Why sacrifice yourself for others?' After a short pause for quiet reflection, I invited an eager young man to start us off by giving his first thoughts. This is what he said:

> It seems to me that 'sacrifice' is the most important concept in this question. I think someone might sacrifice themselves based on instinct, impulse or intuition. Of course, two of these are in the cognitive domain and one is in the affective domain, so I suppose we need to determine which of these is more likely in any given situation before we can answer the question reasonably.

All the other delegates were nodding approvingly at the boy's apparent confidence in thinking about and analysing the concept of sacrifice. As for me, I was like a bunny rabbit caught in the headlights; I certainly had not been expecting that response!

To grab some thinking time for myself, I asked the teenagers to decide what these terms – instinct, impulse and intuition – had in common. While they did that, I begged a friendly philosopher to suggest what I might do next.

Reconvening, I asked one girl to give her group's answer. She will forever be a favourite of mine after replying: 'Instinct, Impulse and Intuition are all names of perfumes.'

Once the hour-long discussion had finished, I made a beeline for the organisers and moaned that they had set me up. 'You could've told me you'd invited only the most talented philosophers from across Bulgaria to join us!' They laughingly explained they had simply invited volunteers from the local area to take part – there hadn't been any selection process.

'So how come they're so adept at thinking?' I inquired. 'Because they've been taught how to think from an early age', they said. 'But so have children in the UK and yet I haven't come across young teenagers as skilled in thinking as your students', I countered. Their response was something that initially vexed, then intrigued and ultimately emboldened me: 'From what we've seen in Western countries, you don't seem to teach children *how* to think; instead you teach them *what* to think.'

The more I work in schools, the more I think these Bulgarian teachers may have been right.

When I ask junior school children whether they think stealing is wrong, they all answer yes. But if I then ask why we think of Robin Hood as having been right, they always retort: 'He robbed from the rich and gave to the poor, which makes it okay.' Perhaps there's nothing too controversial there yet but if I press them to decide if it would be okay for me to steal, let's say from a bank, and give the proceeds to poor people, they always say yes. Rarely do the children seem troubled by the fact that stealing from anybody, no matter what the funds are used for, is against the law.

Cognitive conflict

I wonder if this suggests the Bulgarian teachers might be right – that many children are being taught *what*, rather than *how*, to think?

For example, I often notice teachers and parents praising children for saying the 'right' thing: 'it is wrong to kill'; 'we must always be nice'; 'you should never lie'; and so on. And on the face it, this might seem reasonable. After all, we want children to be moral and to do the right thing. However, what happens if they are faced with a dilemma but, up to that point, have only ever followed instructions? Such dilemmas might include eating meat while maintaining that killing is wrong; always telling the truth even if it is likely to hurt someone; always being nice even to someone being either racist or bullying a friend. What then?

FIGURE 5.1 Cognitive conflict – agreeing with two (or more) opposing ideas

Many parents will reply that they trust their children to do the right thing. But how do children know what the 'right' thing is unless they have learnt how to make moral decisions for themselves? In other words, how can they be moral if they haven't learnt how to think or developed at least some wisdom?

By three methods we may learn wisdom: first, by reflection, which is noblest; second by imitation, which is easiest; and third by experience, which is the bitterest.

(Confucius, 551–479 BC)

Confusion leading to wisdom

One of the best ways to build children's wisdom and moral decision-making is to confuse them! Of course I'm being tongue-in-cheek when I say 'confuse' them. It would be more accurate to say 'help create cognitive conflict in their minds'.

Cognitive conflict is about setting up a conflict of opinions within a person's mind (as opposed to a conflict between two or more people). This conflict, or

FIGURE 5.2 When cognitive conflict goes wrong

dissonance, then unsettles the thinker and causes them to reflect on what it is they actually think.

For example, ask children if it's ever okay to tell lies. They will probably say no. This is thought number one: 'It is wrong to tell lies.' Now ask them if they should lie if their mother asks them whether her bum looks big or if Dad asks them whether his joke was a funny one. This prompts the second thought in their minds: 'It might be better to lie if it makes someone happy.' With older children, you might ask them to think about a doctor lying to a patient, a football manager lying to the television cameras, or them lying to a bully who is seeking out his or her next victim.

This conflict of opinions between thinking that lying is wrong, while also believing that lying is often the best thing to do is what creates the cognitive conflict.

The prime reason for setting up cognitive conflict is that it encourages us to think more. When we know the solution to a problem, we have no need to think about it; we simply solve it and move on. However, when we experience cognitive conflict in our minds, then the tension between the two ideas should cause us to think more deeply.

I call the techniques I use to create cognitive conflict 'wobblers'. These are explored on the following pages.

Wobblers

As I wrote in my book, *Challenging Learning*, wobblers are a great way to create cognitive conflict. Here are the wobblers I use most often.

Wobbler 1: If A = B

This involves asking what something is, taking whatever a child says and then testing it by turning it around and adding an example. For instance:

I ask: What is a pet?

A child responds: An animal you look after.

I then ask: Does that mean if we look after an animal then it is a pet? For example, if I put food out for the birds?

The process looks something like this:

If **A** = B then does B = **A**? (+ example)

A is **the concept that you are considering**, in this case '**pet**'.

B is the child's response, in this case 'An animal you look after'.

The example is whatever disproves the first idea, in this case putting food out for wild birds.

Examples of Wobbler 1

- If bullying (A) means hurting someone (B), then does that mean that if I hurt someone (B) then I'm bullying them (A)?

  For example, if I commit a foul against someone during a sports match? Or I give someone some bad news?

- If a holiday (A) is having a rest (B) then if I have a rest (B), am I on holiday (A)?

  For example, resting on the sofa at the end of the day or every night before I go to bed?

- If a hero (A) is someone who is brave (B), does that mean a brave person (B) is a hero (A)?

  For example, someone who runs across a motorway might be brave but is that person a hero?

- If a number (A) is something we use in maths (B), does that mean something we use in maths (B) is a number (A)?

  For example, a calculator?

Wobbler 2: NOT A

An alternative to the first wobbler is to add a negative. The structure then becomes as shown here.

If **A** = <u>B</u>, then if it's <u>NOT B</u>, is it also **NOT A**?

A is **the thing you are considering**, for example **'friend'**.

<u>B</u> is <u>the child's response</u>, e.g. '<u>someone I play with</u>'.

So this time, to create cognitive conflict, we ask:

Does that mean if you do not play (<u>NOT B</u>) with your friend today that you are not friends (**NOT A**)?

Examples of Wobbler 2

- If children say that fairness (A) is about 'being the same' (B), then if we are not the same (NOT B) then does that mean it is not fair (NOT A)?

  For example, you and I are different because we have different eye colour/hair cut/arm length, etc.

- If a dream (A) is the thinking we do when we're asleep (B) then if I'm not asleep (not B), does that mean I can't dream (not A)?

  For example, the dreams we have when we're half awake or day-dreaming.

Some cautionary notes about Wobblers

Wobblers are not designed to *prove* children wrong. Rather, they are intended to cause people to go beyond the easy answer or first response, to help them identify contradictions and misconceptions, and, ultimately, to develop the habit of questioning their own ideas.

Challenging children's thinking in an attempt to discredit or disprove their hypotheses can be harmful; it is far more productive to be playful with ideas. This helps to develop a sense of co-inquiring rather than an 'I know best' attitude that can be very disheartening. It also draws attention to the reality that adults do not know everything!

This type of challenge could be said to be a form of trickery. Of course, trickery has negative connotations (the trickery of a conman) as well as positive ones (the trickery of a children's magician). These wobblers seek to provide the trickery that is positive, fun and engaging.

On my website, challenginglearning.com, there are a few short videos in which I create cognitive conflict in the minds of children between the ages of three and sixteen. There is also a clip of a keynote speech I gave in York in 2009 in which I explain how and why we might want to create cognitive conflict. In all of these examples, note the sense of mischief and fun, rather than any malice or point-scoring.

Examples of when a child holds two opposing opinions simultaneously:

Opinion A		Opinion B	
1	If I'm bullied I should tell an adult	1	If I'm bullied I should hit back harder
2	Drugs are illegal	2	Drugs are prescribed
3	It is wrong to kill	3	I like to eat meat
4	Animals can't talk	4	Animals talk on the TV
5	You shouldn't call people names	5	It is polite to address a person by their name
6	Don't talk to strangers	6	Go and sit on Santa's knee
7	I should make up my own mind	7	I should do what my elders tell me
8	Many hands make light work	8	Too many cooks spoil the broth
9	A problem shared is a problem halved.	9	Don't tell tales.

The moral purpose of cognitive conflict

A common concern among teachers (and parents) is the incidence of children coasting through school without really having to think for themselves. A similar problem can be noted more generally in children's lives: many youngsters seem able (maybe even encouraged) to live life without dealing with, or even recognising, the dilemmas they face.

The lists above show common examples of conflicting opinions that seem to exist side by side in children's minds.

Many of us might say that's just the way life is – full of dilemmas. However, I think one of the dangers of encouraging our young people to ignore these dilemmas, and countless others, is that we are not helping them to learn when it is right to do as they are told and when it is right to think for themselves.

In other words, there is a danger that by simply doing as they are told – in whatever circumstances – children are not learning to be wise.

For example, say I warn my children that (non-prescription) drugs are dangerous and that they should ignore reports about some drugs being declassified. Perhaps this seems the right thing to do. But what then stops them from being susceptible to agreeing with a drug dealer when he or she advises them to ignore what their parents tell them and to try ecstasy, along with everyone else in the club?

A classic case of cognitive conflict is when teachers insist that children report bullying, whereas many parents (particularly dads) encourage them to hit back instead!

Since there is very little difference in process between these two – both are saying 'ignore one side of the argument' – then what is to stop children developing the sort of shallow thinking that leads to the 'I was told to do it' excuse used by so many defendants at the Nuremburg trials?

I believe the solution to this problem lies, first, in learning how to deal with cognitive conflict in a reasoning, as well as reasonable, manner; and then second to encourage young people to recognise when there is a potential conflict in their thinking and/or actions.

For example, we might begin to initiate cognitive conflict in young children by asking them to decide whether animals can talk or not (bearing in mind animals seem able to communicate, if not talk – although they appear to talk on the

FIGURE 5.3 Teaching children how (not) to deal with bullies

television). With older children we might induce cognitive conflict by prompting them not so much to confirm that bullying is wrong but to consider what it is.

For example:

Idea 1: Bullying is about making someone feel bad.

Idea 2: It would make someone feel bad if I told them their cat had died, but this wouldn't normally be bullying.

Top tips for wisdom

1   Compliment wisdom

Wisdom is extremely difficult to define. Does it have something to do with foresight or hindsight? Is it the same as being clever? Does it only ever come with age and experience? Having just glanced at the dictionary on my desk, there are eleven different definitions of the word and that is just according to *Chambers Dictionary*.

Thankfully, as Wittgenstein once pointed out, just because we can't define something doesn't mean we don't recognise it when we see it. (See p. 117 for more details.)

One of the best ways to help children become wiser is to draw attention to wisdom in practice. For example, compliment it when you notice it: 'that was a wise thing to do' (rather than 'that was a good thing to do'); encourage it by saying 'be wise' when children head off unaccompanied; or share your deliberations as you try to decide what the wisest choice might be.

2   Think through concepts

A concept – e.g. city – is a general idea that groups things together according to accepted characteristics. The practice of conceptual analysis provides many opportunities for deep thinking and discussion with children. Important concepts that children ought to understand include truth, justice, difference, opinion, decision, evidence, number, thought and culture.

In the next chapter, I write about the *Learning Challenge* as a way to boost children's self-esteem. This model is also an excellent way to engage children in thinking about concepts.

Through a process of creating cognitive conflict (referred to as 'the pit' of the *Learning Challenge*), children begin to wonder about and question the meanings and applications of particular concepts.

There are more examples of this process in Chapter 7 and online at p4c.com as well as encouraginglearning.com.

3 Dabble with P4C

Philosophy for Children (P4C) is a worldwide educational movement developed by Matthew Lipman and practised in more than sixty countries. It does not intend to turn children into mini-philosophers; rather, it helps them to become more thoughtful, reflective, considerate and reasonable people. Of all the approaches to learning I know of, P4C continues to be my greatest love.

I mention more in Chapter 7 and online at p4c.com. I highly recommend that you at least dabble in P4C with your children.

Boost your children's self-esteem

Self-esteem is not something we give to people by telling them about their high intelligence. It is something we equip them to get for themselves – by teaching them to value learning over the appearance of smartness, to relish challenge and effort, and to use errors as routes to mastery.

(Dweck, 2006)[34]

Self-esteem coin

Positives including:

- How successful I think I've been
- How successful I think I will be in the future
- How popular I think I am
- How good I think I look
- How much influence I think I have

Resilience including:

- How well I have dealt with problems in the past
- How resilient I think I will be in the future
- How I think I can cope by myself
- How positively I respond to lack of influence or power

FIGURE 6.1 The two sides of self-esteem

Positives including:

- Feelings of success
- Feelings of popularity
- Feelings of beauty
- Feelings of influence

Resilience including:

- Dealing with problems
- Changing outcomes
- Feelings of coping well
- Changing outcomes

Introduction

Although 'self-esteem' is sometimes thought of as a modern-day obsession, John Milton wrote about the concept as far back as 1657. Modern-day definitions are often considered as 'footnotes to the work of William James', who wrote about the concept in his book *The Consciousness of Self* in 1890. Interestingly, James defined self-esteem as 'a ratio found by dividing a person's success in life by their failures in life'.[35]

I defined self-esteem in my earlier book, *Challenging Learning*, in this way:

> Self-esteem is a balance between success and failure; it is a combination of how successful a person thinks they have been/will be, together with how they think they have coped/will cope with setbacks and failure.[36]

In this sense, self-esteem is rather like a two-sided coin as shown opposite. On one side, there are the features normally associated with self-esteem, including feelings of success, popularity and influence. The flipside includes resilience, determination and being able to cope with failure.

This being the case, there are implications for how we interact with children. If we only ever help them to succeed (and praise them for doing so), then they will struggle to develop the resilience side of 'their coin'. Similarly, if children only ever experience failure and problems, then they will become easily discouraged and rarely develop the topside of their coin.

Another couple of theories worth considering in this context come from Maslow and Bandura.

Maslow's 'Hierarchy of Needs' was presented in 1943 and proposed a hierarchy of five levels of basic needs: physiological (e.g. food, drink, shelter), safety (e.g. health, money, resources), belonging (e.g. love, affection, roots), esteem (explored below) and self-actualisation (achieving one's potential). Maslow believed that a person would not feel the second need (safety) until the demands of the first need (physiological) have been satisfied, nor the third until the second has been satisfied, and so on.

Within the esteem level, he noted two versions: a lower one and a higher one. The lower is the need for the respect of others, status, recognition, fame, prestige and attention. The higher is the need for self-esteem, strength, competence, mastery, self-confidence, independence and freedom. It is interesting how many people appear to crave fame and recognition when self-esteem and mastery are, according to Maslow, a higher form of esteem.

Whether Maslow's model accurately reflects real life is open to debate, particularly given that many of the world's most spiritual individuals are also among the poorest people, with the lowest physiological and safety levels. Nonetheless, it is a useful model in that it rightly places self-esteem within a context of other human needs.

Some people prefer to use the term self-efficacy, rather than self-esteem, because of its clearer link with overcoming obstacles. Proposed by Stanford psychologist Albert Bandura in the 1970s, self-efficacy is a judgement that a person has specific capabilities that will lead to success (as opposed to self-esteem, which is used to describe a feeling of self-worth).

Either way, whether we are talking about self-esteem or self-efficacy, an absolutely necessary ingredient is challenge.

There is a danger in trying to protect children from challenges, obstacles and even failure because this can end up *lowering* their self-esteem. To counteract this, I have designed the *Learning Challenge*. This model is described over the next few pages and shows one way to develop children's self-esteem and vital resilience.

Self-esteem and the *Learning Challenge*

The *Learning Challenge* is one way to develop children's self-esteem and resilience. It is a model I developed from the original work of John Edwards and Jim Butler[37] and shows how we might think more deeply about particular concepts. The process involves going into a *Learning Pit* and, in so doing, increase resilience and tenacity, both of which are vital aspects of self-esteem.

The four stages of the *Learning Challenge* are:

CONCEPT (p. 81 and also on p. 87)

CONFLICT (p. 87)

CONSTRUCT (p. 92)

CONSIDER (pp. 97–8).

The four stages of the *Learning Challenge*

Here are the four stages of the *Learning Challenge*. The model has applications for education, the workplace and home.

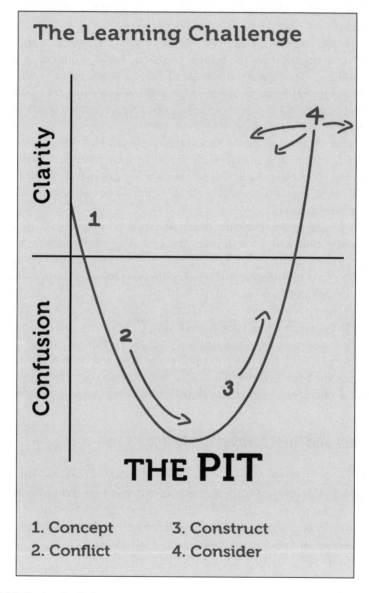

FIGURE 6.2 The *Learning Challenge*

Stage 1: Concept

The *Learning Challenge* begins with a concept. As I described on p. 81, a concept is a general idea that groups things together according to accepted characteristics. For example, the concept of 'capital cities' goes deeper than the straightforward fact that Paris is the capital of France.

Concepts can come from the media, conversation, observations or deliberate study. Good examples to begin with include:

Art, democracy, evidence, fairness, food, good, growth, happiness, love, money, names, number, theory and truth.

Stage 2: Conflict

As soon as a concept has been agreed, Stage 2 is about creating cognitive conflict. As shown on pp. 74–5, cognitive conflict arises from having at least two opinions, both of which we agree with, but that are in conflict with each other. For example, I agree that stealing is wrong but I also think that Robin Hood was a good man; or that truth is something that I believe to be true but that I could be telling the truth even when I'm intending to lie (for example, the mouse in the story of *The Gruffalo* thinks he is making up the existence of a *Gruffalo* – and therefore lying – even though he later discovers that there really *is* a *Gruffalo* in the woods).

Below, you'll see an example of how cognitive conflict can be created. The following dialogues reflect real-life discussions I have had with children in schools:

Key to notation:
    (**1**) – concept is identified
    (**2**) – challenge begins
    (**E**) – Eureka moment (see p. 92).

In both of the following dialogues, the concept is marked with (**1**) and the beginnings of cognitive conflict with (**2**).

Please be assured that I am not trying to score points or to belittle the children in any sense; that would be socially (if not morally) suspect as well as counter-productive. Instead, I am aiming to get the young people thinking *more* by temporarily blocking their normal answers and, in so doing, developing their insights and deepening their resilience.

For example, if I were to ask some children what an odd number is and then accept the first answer ('can't be divided by two'), how much thought would have been required on their part? They've already learned the answer and so can respond almost mechanically.

The *Learning Challenge* with seven-year-olds:

ME:	Two, seven and eight: which number is different from the other two and why?
ANDREW:	Seven, because it's an odd number. **(1)**
ME:	What's an odd number?
CAROLINE:	A number that can't be divided by two.
ME:	So, if I have £7, are you saying it can't be divided by two? How much would each person have if I shared £7 between two people? **(2)**
CHARLOTTE:	£3.50 each.
ME:	So, seven can be divided by two. Does that mean it's even then? **(2)**
SERGEI:	No!
ME:	So what is an odd number?
SERGEI:	It can't be divided by two without leaving a remainder.
ME:	But when I divided £7 by two, that didn't leave a remainder.
DANIEL:	But 50p is not a whole number. You can't divide an odd number by two without splitting a whole number.
ME:	Are you telling me that fifty is not a whole number? **(2)**
SUNITA:	50 pence isn't.
ME:	This (holding a 50p piece) is not whole? Why not? It looks whole to me.
SUNITA:	But it's not a whole pound. It's half of a pound.
ME:	So, what is an odd number then?
BEN:	It's a number that can't be divided by two without changing the units. **(E)**
ME:	Can you give me an example?
BEN:	If I had seven pound coins then I'd have to split one of them in half first.
ME:	Does that mean anything I have to split in half, so that I can share it, is odd?
BEN:	Yes.
ME:	But what if I have a £10 note? I would have to split that to share it wouldn't I? Does that make £10 odd?
BEN:	Um. . . .

The *Learning Challenge* with fourteen-year-olds

What is courage?

ME:	What is courage? **(1)**
JONNY:	Being brave.
ME:	Okay, so what does 'being brave' mean?
SARAH:	Facing your fears.
ME:	But if I'm scared to run across a motorway, but still do it, am I being brave? **(2)**
ELLIE:	No, that's just stupid. You have to do something good to be brave.
ME:	Such as kill someone?
KYLE:	That's not good.
ME:	But lots of soldiers have been awarded medals for bravery and presumably many of them killed the enemy while 'being brave'. **(2)**
KYLE:	Yes, but that was their job.
ME:	So, if I do my job, am I being brave? I'm doing my job now – does that mean I'm being brave? **(2)**
VIJAY:	No, sir. You're not doing your job. You're just trying to confuse us.

(It was very tempting to ask why Vijay thought trying to confuse (or challenge) him wasn't the job of a teacher, but I wanted to stick to the topic.)

ME:	So, if you're just doing your job then you're not being brave; is that right?
SUNITA:	What about firemen? They're brave.
MOLLY:	My Dad's a fireman and all he does is sit around playing computer games.
ME:	But presumably your Dad also rescues people and puts out fires when he's asked to.
MOLLY:	Of course!
ME:	So is he brave then?
MOLLY:	Yeah, I guess.
ME:	Can anyone else tell me what it is about Molly's Dad's job that means he has to be brave to do it?
BEN:	He puts the lives of others before himself.

ME:	Okay, but most mothers seem to put the lives of their kids, or at least the needs of their kids, before their own. Does that mean they're brave? **(2)**
RACHEL:	No, they're stupid. Why give up everything for your kids?
ME:	There's that word again: 'stupid'. It sounds to me as if being brave is about being stupid. Is that right?
PUPILS:	Not really.
ME:	So what does it mean then?
PUPILS:	Why don't you tell us?

Take another example: 'What is a holiday?' I often use this example when I am explaining The *Learning Challenge* to parents and typically the first response is 'not working'. If I were simply to say 'Excellent, thank you', then how much thought would be needed? Instead, I generally reply: 'So if I take a break, for example a coffee break, am I on holiday?' 'No, a holiday is about going away somewhere.' 'But if I don't go away does that mean I can't be on holiday?' 'OK, well it's about taking a break from your routine.' And again I respond with a wobbler (see pp. 77–9), 'But don't we have routines on holiday – for example, child care duties, eating, washing and so on?'

This sense of wobble can be described as being 'in the pit'. The children I've taught liked to say they were in the pit when they had a dilemma and it has since become a popular phrase with teachers I have worked with, too.

The *Learning Pit* and self-esteem

A few years ago, I was having a drink in my local pub, the Red Lion in Alnmouth (check it out – it has real ales, roaring fires and a great atmosphere). After a while I felt the call of nature and headed for the gents, but was somewhat startled by a voice saying: 'Hello, sir. Remember me?'

I didn't know what to do – run, hide or beg for mercy. Thankfully though, it turned out to be an ex-pupil of mine, Gary, who I'd always got along well with. He was all grown up by then so I bought him a pint and we had a chat that went something like this:

'So how's life treating you these days, Gary?'
'Ever since I left school things have been much better.'
'Why didn't you like school?'
'You know that pit you taught us about? Well I spent my life in that bloody pit. The teachers would start waffling on, I'd get all confused and then they'd say, "so moving on then". I used to think, don't move on – I'm still in the pit!'

'Did you hate everything about school?'

'No, I loved the lessons where you got us all into the pit.'

'But you said you hated being in the pit.'

'I did when I was by myself but when everyone else was in the pit, I thought "welcome to my world, let me show you around".'

After that, Gary told me about leaving school with no qualifications. He started his own window-cleaning business that now employs more than twenty people. As I quizzed him about his life story, it struck me just how much determination, resilience and belief in himself (or self-esteem) he possessed. I wonder if that had anything to do with his life *in the pit*?

James Heckman, Nobel Prize winner and adviser to President Obama, argued in a lecture in London[38] that governments in developed countries are mistaken in focussing primarily on children's cognitive skills when, arguably, character development is more important. He uses an acronym, OCEAN – taken from the Big Five framework of personality traits from Costa and McCrae, 1992, to capture the main characteristics of successful people: Openness (being willing to learn); Conscientiousness (staying on task); Extroversion (being outgoing and friendly); Agreeableness (being helpful); and Neuroticism (persisting and paying attention to detail).

Of course, this is a fairly USA-centric view. For example, in the UK we might wish to see humour mentioned somewhere; in India something to do with introversion (being self-aware) might be preferable to extroversion.

My reason for mentioning Heckman is not to agree a definitive list of characteristics but to show that (a) personal qualities should not be overlooked, and (b) that such virtues tend to be developed in the pit.

Ensuring the *Learning Challenge* works

Sticking to the following principles will ensure that the *Learning Challenge* works for you, particularly to build self-esteem and resilience. Each item mentions children but the pit is just as useful for adults, particularly in a work context:

1   Children are generally more interested in learning when others around them are curious and willing to express uncertainty. The *Learning Challenge* therefore assumes a willingness to say, 'I'm not sure', or 'I'm confused'.

2   We are all fallible. The *Learning Challenge* assumes we are willing to admit, or even draw attention to, our own errors.

3   High quality learning comes from making connections and understanding relationships between ideas. Being in the pit compels us to make these links.

4   Everyone taking part in the *Learning Challenge* should aim to be thoughtful, reflective, supportive and reasonable.

5   Though most instances of the *Learning Challenge* result in agreement about what answers are 'right', there are occasions, particularly with philosophical questions, when no right answer is achievable. This does not make the experience any less valid. It is the *process* of thinking together, reflecting and giving reasons that is at the heart of learning.

Stage 3: Construct

While struggling in the pit together, we begin to create better answers.

A good example of this can be seen on p. 88 during the dialogue with seven-year-olds. While investigating odd numbers and getting ourselves deeply into a pit, one of the boys, who incidentally had 'dyscalculia' (difficulties with understanding numbers) said: 'I've got it; it's like odd socks, isn't it?'

I asked him to explain further: 'My mother reckons that no matter how many socks she puts in the washing machine, she always gets an odd number out.' 'What do you mean?' I asked. 'She takes them out, dries them and lays them out on the kitchen table. Then she takes one, puts it together with another and folds them. She does this until always at the end, there's one left over. Odd numbers are like that, aren't they?'

It was at this point that three children recently arrived from Poland had their 'aha' moment. Up to that point, they had been a little lost with what was going on, mainly because of the speed of conversation. But when they heard Darren describe his mother's odd socks, they instantly knew what he was talking about. Perhaps the same phenomenon can be seen with Polish socks in the wash.

This anecdote nicely describes some of the key features of the *Learning Challenge*: (1) children help each other to learn; (2) knowledge constructed through social interaction is often far more meaningful than knowledge that is served up on a plate by the teacher or parent; (3) children who 'teach' others are more likely to remember information in the long term than those who are 'taught'; (4) this sort of challenging dialogue often provokes 'Eureka' moments.

To teach is to learn twice.

(Joseph Joubert, 1754–1824)

The 'Eureka' moment

Eureka is the key to the *Learning Challenge*. After struggling in the pit for a while, eventually we see the light and enjoy a Eureka moment – the point when we realise the effort has been worthwhile and that it feels great to be 'in the know'.

Incidentally, the Eureka moment in each of the dialogues on pp. 88–90 is marked with an (E).

FIGURE 6.3 Eureka – Greek for 'I found it'

When children experience the Eureka moment, they want to share it with everybody. They talk and talk and talk about it – and then want to do it again. Contrast this with the typical response we get when we ask our children what they did at school that day: 'nothing!'

In June 2007, I was giving a keynote speech at a conference in Sweden and mentioned the Eureka moment. At that moment, a woman in the audience jumped up and declared that she'd just been married! Baffled, I inquired as to the relevance of such a statement. She then revealed (to the 600 people in the auditorium) that her new husband was Greek so she'd been learning Greek, and that 'Eureka' was Greek for 'I found it'.

Though bemused by the new Mrs Papadopoulos's outburst, I was also very interested in this meaning of Eureka. It doesn't mean 'my Dad gave me the answer' or that 'Grandma told me how to do it'. Eureka means 'I found it'.

It seems to me this is what the ecstasy of learning is all about: if we persevere with a problem until we hit upon a solution then we get a wonderful sense of achievement and a feeling that we have an almost-unique insight into the *real* meaning of the concept. And this feeling only comes when we overcome challenges. It does not come from understanding something quickly or easily.

Eureka is dependent upon first struggling. We have to get in the pit first if we are to enjoy a sense of achievement later.

Your Eureka moments

For further insight into Eureka moments, please take some time to think and/or talk about these questions:

1   How often did you experience Eureka moments during your own school days?
2   How did you feel the last time you experienced a Eureka moment?

3   What difference did it make to your understanding of the subject?

4   Did it affect your attitude towards learning? If so, how?

5   How often do your children experience their own Eureka moments?

6   What could you do to enhance the quality and quantity of Eureka moments for your children?

> Kites rise against the wind, not with it.
>
> (Winston Churchill, 1874–1965)

FIGURE 6.4 Churchill's kite

Strategies for climbing out of the pit

I'm often asked to recommend ways to help children out of the pit. Parents (and teachers) find it quite easy to confuse their children but helping children construct meaning without simply giving them the answer appears to be much more complex.

First of all, I'd say use the term 'in the pit' and share the idea of the *Learning Challenge* with your children. This will help create a shared language to use when dealing with cognitive conflict.

At this point, I should say the pit does *not* represent the occasions when we have *no* idea – for example, I have no idea about the 'Higgs boson' that scientists are trying to prove exists. Instead, the pit represents those times when we hold *at least two* ideas simultaneously that seem to conflict. For instance, we think that equality is right but we also think that one group of people should be given preference over another; we think we should never tell lies but we also know that telling lies can be the right thing to do at times.

So the next time your children are experiencing cognitive conflict tell them that they are 'in the pit' and remind them that this is a necessary part of learning. Then, once they have been in the pit for a while – in other words, do *not* rush in as if you were a 'helicopter parent' (see p. 8) – suggest that they try one of the following strategies for constructing a suitable answer.

A Common characteristics

It may be useful to think back to some examples of inner conflict that I outlined earlier. We might struggle to define precisely what a holiday is but we certainly know when we experience one; we might not be able to say for sure why names are important but we certainly know how we feel when people get our names wrong. This is what Ludwig Wittgenstein (1889–1951), one of the twentieth century's most important philosophers, meant when he wrote that just because we can't define something doesn't mean to say we don't recognise it when we see it.

Take the concept of courage. We might think that it's about being brave but then think of an example when that is more foolhardy than courageous (e.g. playing chicken on a railway line). Or we might think that it is about risking oneself for the greater good but then feel uncomfortable agreeing that terrorists are courageous although they risk themselves for what *they* see as the greater good.

What Wittgenstein would suggest is that we first select cases of the concept in action, such as the courage demonstrated by fire fighters, soldiers, Grace Darling, the Suffragettes, or someone who stands up to a bully. Then we identify the characteristics these examples have in common, such as putting themselves at risk, considering others before themselves, standing up for what they believe in, believing that they can change things. Finally, we create a conclusion that, although not perfect, is almost certainly more complete and thought-through than our initial answer.

B Hierarchy

A popular way to sift through the myriad of possible answers that children come up with in the pit is to rank them. This can be done in a diamond shape, as shown on p. 96 (and recommended on p. 63), or in a straight line, or a pyramid. So long as children analyse the relative value of each answer, it should help them to distinguish which combination of their earlier responses would generate the best compound (or overall) answer.

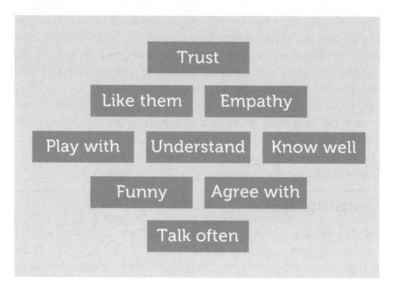

FIGURE 6.5 Diamond ranking different aspects of friendship

C Relationships

Another way to help children climb out of the pit is to encourage them to describe the concept they are analysing in relation to another concept.

For example:

- How does a friend differ from a best friend?
- Is cowardice always the opposite of courage?
- How do knowledge and wisdom differ?
- Is faith different to belief?
- How is 'fake' different from 'make-believe'?

Sometimes it can be productive to compare the concept you are thinking about with another concept that is chosen at random, as this often leads to unexpected discoveries.

For example:

- courage and honesty;
- lying and dreams;
- odd numbers and zoos;
- thinking and racism;
- art and mind.

NB. As I discovered when my first book was translated into Norwegian, we have far more words in English than in most other languages (because we have, among others, Germanic, French, Norse, Latin *and* Greek words). This means we have far more opportunity for comparing concepts with synonyms – so make use of them!

D Categorise

Venn diagrams are useful as a thinking tool and not just in school maths. They can help us to categorise and to distinguish between two (or more) inter-related concepts. The activity on p. 69 makes use of a Venn diagram.

For example, if your children are attempting to define the nature of friendship, but are getting bogged down with the similarity with 'being friendly', then a Venn diagram such as this might help:

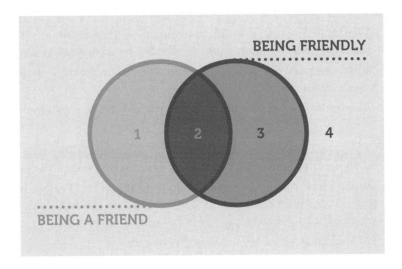

FIGURE 6.6 Using Venn diagrams to explore concepts

By identifying the characteristics that apply only to Area 1, your children will be able to describe more accurately the essential characteristics of 'being a friend'.

Stage 4: Consider

The fourth and final part of the *Learning Challenge* is to think back over each stage of the pit. This will help children to recognise the progress they have made in their thinking and to decide which strategies they might use again in the future.

In his book, on *Unified Theories of Cognition*, Allen Newell points out that there are two layers of problem solving: the first is solving the problem; the second is being aware of the strategies used. Good problem solving, Newell observed, often depends as much on the selection and monitoring of a strategy as on its execution.[39] More and more, the term *metacognition* (thinking about thinking) is used to refer to this process of selection and monitoring strategies that all good thinking requires.

Here are some useful metacognitive questions to use when thinking about the *Learning Challenge*:

Stage 1

(a) What did you think the concept meant initially (and why do you think you thought that)?

(b) What definitions did you hear others use?

(c) What were the best bits and/or weaknesses of your first idea?

Stage 2

(d) How did you feel as you entered the pit?

(e) What caused you to question your first idea? (For example: 'When I realised that saying odd numbers *cannot* be divided by two was too simplistic.')

(f) What strategies did you use to deal with your feelings of uncertainty and frustration in the pit?

(g) Which ideas or answers did you reject while in the pit and why?

Stage 3

(h) What was the best strategy you used for climbing out of the pit and why?

(i) Which ideas make most sense to you now and why? (For example: 'The idea that odd numbers can be divided by two but we say they can't because when divided they never result in a whole number answer.')

(j) How did that sense of Eureka make you feel?

Stage 4

(k) How does your new answer differ from your earlier ideas?

(l) Which strategies would you use the next time you find yourself in the pit?

(m) How do you feel about learning now that you've been into the pit and climbed out the other side?

(n) What analogy, metaphor or example could you use now to explain this concept to someone else?

> If you can't explain it simply, you don't understand it well enough.
>
> (Albert Einstein, 1875–1955)

Praise and the pit

Connecting with the earlier chapter about praise (see pp. 36–53), here is what I recommend in terms of praise for each stage of the pit:

Stage 1

Try to avoid praise at this initial stage. Show interest in children's first answers, of course, and pleasure that they have at least responded, but try not to say 'well done' or 'excellent'. At the most, say (with a smile) 'thank you' or 'interesting idea'. Avoiding early praise will encourage children to persevere.

Stage 2

Now is the time to praise! Praise children's tenacity and resolution. Say how impressed you are that they are willing to explore and challenge their own ideas. In short, remind them that the pit is a necessary part of noteworthy learning and that you are delighted they are willing to withstand challenges.

Stage 3

At this stage, use phrases such as 'I bet you feel good about thinking your way through the pit', or 'you should be proud of yourself for sticking at it – now enjoy your Eureka moment!' Notice that I'm suggesting we encourage more internal praise, rather than allowing our children to become over-reliant on external affirmations.

Stage 4

This is a good stage at which to encourage your children to think how they felt throughout the process, what they might do differently next time and how they can achieve more by seeking out and overcoming challenges.

Self-esteem, Dweck mindsets and the *Learning Challenge*

In *The Six Pillars of Self-esteem* by Nathaniel Branden, there is an exploration of the different characteristics of people with low self-esteem, compared to those with high self-esteem.[40] On the next page is a summary of some of those.

Notice the similarities between the typical behaviour of people with low self-esteem shown opposite and the behaviours associated with people of a fixed mindset shown on p. 34–5: both are wary of change; both seem to prefer to prove, rather than *im*prove themselves; and both are more likely to be frustrated by challenges.

Whereas the similarities in behaviour between those with high self-esteem and people with a growth mindset (shown on p. 35) include tending to have more coping strategies; being more open to new situations as well as to change; and choosing growth and expression over playing it safe or showing off to others.

People with low self-esteem tend to be:	People with high self-esteem tend to be:
1 rigid in their thinking	1 flexible in their thinking
2 fearful of new and unfamiliar situations	2 keen to experience new situations
3 wary of change	3 open to change
4 cautious of other people	4 cooperative with others
5 keen to prove themselves	5 keen to express themselves
6 reassured by the familiar	6 excited by challenge
7 evasive in what they say	7 honest in what they say
8 more likely to give up	8 more persistent
9 easily frustrated	9 tolerant
10 less equipped to cope.	10 quicker to recover.

So it seems the link between self-esteem and Dweck's theory of mindset is very close indeed. It also poses the question: which comes first, self-esteem or a growth mindset? (I'd suggest it is a chicken or egg situation.)

Furthermore, look at the behaviours associated with high self-esteem, a growth mindset and the traits you would expect children to develop in the *Learning Pit*: resilience, determination, curiosity, being more open to challenges, and so on. Again, the links seem to be very clear: if we wish to help our children develop positive learning attitudes, then we need to encourage them to seek out challenges and situations similar to those typified by the *Learning Challenge*.

Finally, if we want all this for our children, then we'll have far more success if we are *also* willing to get in *the Pit!*

Top tips for boosting self-esteem

1 Self-esteem affects learning

Although it is almost impossible to determine an exact causal link between self-esteem and achievement, it seems apparent that the best learners have high self-esteem and that the worst have low self-esteem.

2 Self-esteem has a resilience dimension

Children's self-esteem is not reliant solely on believing they have been and will be successful; it is also dependent on knowing they can cope with setbacks and failure and that they are resilient learners/people.

3   Self-esteem and challenge: a chicken or egg scenario

To develop high levels of self-esteem, children need to know they can overcome challenges but, often, they are unwilling to tackle challenging circumstances unless they have high levels of self-confidence.

4   Inner strength is a higher form of esteem than prestige or fame

According to Maslow's 'Hierarchy of Needs', there is a lower form of esteem involving recognition by others, status and even fame, whereas a higher form of esteem involves inner strength and independent thought. It is this higher form that Maslow refers to as self-esteem.

5   Praise determination, effort and hard work

If we always praise children for getting things right, regardless of the levels of challenge, then the message they receive is that we value correct answers far more than a willingness to grow and learn. Instead, praise effort and hard work.

6   Indirect praise can sometimes be more effective

If you want children to improve, let them overhear the nice things you say about them to others (Ginott, 2004).[41] In doing so, you reduce the chance of them wondering if your praise is artificial.

7   The *Learning Challenge* can help build resilience and self-esteem (in adults as well as children)

I have shared the *Learning Challenge* with almost every class of children I've taught. The stages and ideas behind it became a shared language. Phrases such as 'I'm in the pit' or 'I don't understand why some people are in the pit when I'm still at Stage 1' were commonplace.

   This not only led to a greater understanding of the learning process for all concerned, but also built my pupils' capacity for learning and their willingness to take up challenges. As Matthew Lipman, the creator of Philosophy for Children (see Chapter 7) once wrote: 'We need more challenge and less instruction, since it is from challenge that one grows in body, mind and spirit.'[42]

7

Curiosity did *not* kill the cat

Curiosity is the very basis of education and if you tell me that curiosity killed the cat, I say only the cat died nobly.

(Arnold Edinborough, 1922–2006)

FIGURE 7.1 Curiosity did *not* kill the cat

Introduction

I remember, as a young child, being disdainful of the phrase 'Curiosity killed the cat'. I probably could not have told you why I didn't like it – I just felt it was a stupid thing to say. My aversion grew every time somebody used the phrase to deflect what I thought was an interesting and purposeful question.

So imagine how exonerated I felt when I discovered that curiosity did *not* kill the cat! Apparently it was 'care' (as in worry or nervousness) that sent the cat on its way.

The original phrase, was used in 1598 by Ben Johnson in the play *Every Man in His Humour*:

> Helter skelter, hang sorrow, care will kill a cat, up-tails all and a pox on the Hangman.

The following year, Shakespeare used a similar phrase in *Much Ado About Nothing*:

> What, courage man! What though care killed a cat, thou hast mettle enough in thee to kill care.

According to *Wikipedia*: 'The earliest known printed reference to the actual phrase 'Curiosity killed the cat' is in James Allan Mair's 1873 compendium: *A Handbook of Proverbs*, where it is listed as an Irish proverb on page 34.'[43]

However, regardless of the origins, I think it is high time we rid ourselves of this silly saying. Without curiosity, we wouldn't have the inventions we do today, there'd be no advances in medicine and new and exciting ideas would be few and far between. So I say, let us celebrate, encourage and teach curiosity. Of course some people might say children are naturally curious and therefore don't need to be taught curiosity. I'm not so sure that is true.

Curious children

> No one asks how to motivate a baby. A baby naturally explores everything it can get at, unless restraining forces have already been at work. And this tendency doesn't die out, it's wiped out.
>
> (B. F. Skinner, 1948, in his novel, *Walden Two*)

Remember, when your children were very young, how curious and imaginative they were? However, they then started school and a decline began to set in; they started answering questions about what they did at school with 'not much' or 'nothing'. Eventually, I'm told, they will most likely become monosyllabic, grunting teenagers before turning twenty and laying the blame for all their maladjustments squarely at their parents' feet.

Well, when my children blame me, I'm going to blame schools.

Children tend to be happy, inquisitive, playful creatures when they are very young. It is only when they start school and discover a structured environment that conforms to a bell, a series of lessons that often don't link together let alone link to real life, and a classroom language that is dictated by the curriculum, that their curiosity begins to wane.

To be fair, when teachers do try to shake things up, many people beat their chests about 'loony liberals' running the classroom. Yet if teachers stick with tradition, other critics are aghast that schools still resemble Victorian factories. No wonder every new government tries to shake things up but ultimately schools rarely change.

There is another inconvenient truth to wreck any argument that schools are to blame: our children spend only 20 per cent of their waking hours in school! (I show the calculation I used to come to this conclusion on p. 126 if you're interested.) So if children spend such a small proportion of their time at school, then what goes on, or perhaps doesn't go on, outside school must also be to blame.

My hunch is that parents' eagerness to help children excel at school often leads to a dampening of their youngsters' curiosity and creativity. This is particularly the case if we put the majority of our efforts into focussing children's attention on knowing right answers, on getting ten out of ten in their tests, or in memorising lots of information. I'm not saying that accuracy is a bad thing – far from it – but a child who isn't encouraged to use this memorised information to investigate and question the world around them will be the poorer for it. Or as Stephen Fry puts it in his autobiography, *The Fry Chronicles*:

> There are young men and women up and down the land who happily (or unhappily) tell anyone who will listen that they don't have an academic turn of mind, or that they aren't lucky enough to have been blessed with a good memory and yet can recite hundreds of pop lyrics and reel off any amount of information about footballers. Why? Because they are interested in those things. They are curious. If you are hungry for food, you are prepared to hunt high and low for it. If you are hungry for information it is the same. Information is all around us, now more than ever before in human history. You barely have to stir or incommode yourself to find things out. The only reason people do not know much is because they do not care to know. They are incurious. Incuriosity is the oddest and most foolish failing there is.[44]

Of course, many parents choose schools that *emphasise* curiosity through a 'creative curriculum' or organise out-of-school activities that encourage creativity. So I'm not suggesting nothing is being done to boost artistry.

However, what I am suggesting is that we could *also* modify our conversations and our day-to-day interactions with our children so that their imagination, curiosity, enterprise and reflection are boosted.

Philosophy for Children[45] is one of the best ways I know for enhancing children's curiosity.

Philosophy holds a key to curiosity

I used to think that philosophy was for people who would rather prevaricate than take action or for those who don't notice how they look and seem to resist getting a proper job. Then I was introduced to Philosophy for Children at the tender age of twenty-one.

Ever since then, I've been a fan of the big 'Ph'.

I don't want to sound as if I have had some sort of evangelical moment or that I'm going to turn up on your doorstep with an invitation to join my cult. However, I *am* convinced of the virtues of philosophy and believe it would be wise to promote philosophical thinking in our schools and homes.

Philosophy is unlike other subjects in two important respects. First, philosophical issues take us to the heart of other subjects. For example, questions about fairness are at the core of geography; evidence is central to science; communication is integral to the study of language. Indeed, this centrality is reflected in the various branches of philosophy – philosophy of ethics, politics, childhood, language, aesthetics and epistemology (theory of knowledge).

Second, philosophy is specifically concerned with good thinking. Of course, good thinking is an art rather than the straightforward application of a set of tools. Yet, just as the most accomplished chef learned the art of cooking through the practice of following recipes accurately, so it is with thinking. Over the next twenty pages or so, there is a 'recipe' for good thinking.

> Over the last week or so we've been asking you for ideas about what subjects ought to be taught in schools but are not taught. Now, there have been many suggestions . . . but the overwhelming winner – you may be surprised by this – was philosophy.
>
> (John Humphrys)[46]

Philosophy for children

In the late 1960s, Matthew Lipman founded the Philosophy for Children project (P4C). His intention was to emphasise many of the values of philosophy – wisdom, reflection, reasoning and reasonableness – and to ensure that they were part of every child's education. Since then, P4C has been developed in more than sixty countries worldwide, has been well researched and proved to be an extremely positive approach to teaching and learning.

To read more about the principles and history of Philosophy for Children, you could visit www.p4c.com, a resource and collaboration cooperative supporting P4C across the world.

P4C offers the best set of strategies I know of for developing the art of good thinking with children.

The basics of P4C

1 Sit in a circle

When setting up a P4C dialogue with a group, it is always best to sit in a circle. This indicates that everyone will be thinking *together* – as opposed to listening to one person, or viewing a screen.

2 Consider a story, picture or other stimulus

Philosophy (and curiosity) begins in wonder. If you can find something that has no obvious answer, no particular moral, or something that is baffling in some way, then it will probably prove to be a good starting point for philosophical inquiry with children. For example:

Artwork

Almost anything will do but particularly work by Pablo Picasso, Banksy, Rita Pearce, or my personal favourite for encouraging inquiry with children – Keith Haring (see www.haringkids.com).

Picture books

Most books have an array of themes that could provoke curiosity. Sure-fire winners include stories by Julia Donaldson, Anthony Browne, David McKee, Edward Monkton or Shaun Tan.

Video stories

I have created a playlist on YouTube that includes some of my favourite stories to begin a thoughtful discussion with children. Search for *Videos for P4C Inquiries* on my YouTube channel: 'jabulani4'.

3 Draw out the main concepts

As I explored on p. 81, a concept – e.g. justice – is a general idea that groups things together according to accepted characteristics. Important concepts that children would do well to understand, include:

Arts

Beauty, art, imagination, reproduction, real, copy, meaning.

Citizenship

Rights, duties, justice, fairness, freedom, welfare, community, enterprise.

Design

Purpose, economy, value, elegance, simplicity, effectiveness, originality.

Humanities/social studies

Justice, globalisation, nation, interpretation, history, truth, cause.

ICT

Knowledge, entertainment, game, reality, legality, morality, social media.

Literature

Love, democracy, fairness, justice, goodness, power, anger.

Religious education

Belief, faith, truth, morality, tolerance, customs, rites.

Science

Science, experiment, evidence, knowledge, theory, fair test, proof, cause, reaction.

4 Create philosophical questions

Some of the more famous philosophical questions include: What is the meaning of life? Is there a god? Is torture justifiable? If a tree falls but no-one hears it, then did it make a sound?

However, there are an almost limitless number of philosophical questions and these can be created from almost any concept. Below are some of the most useful question stems. If you or your children select a concept and then precede it with one of the following question stems, you are likely to create a thought-provoking, philosophical question worth investigating.

Useful question stems are:

- What is . . .
  Example: What is love?

- What makes . . .
  Example: What makes a friend special?

- Would you be . . .
  Example: Would you be the same person if you had a different name?

- How do we know what . . .
  Example: How do we know what courage is?

- Always or never
  Example: Should we *always* obey the law?

- What if . . .
  Example: What if people had never learned how to tell lies?

- Is it possible . . .
  Example: Is it possible to be normal and different at the same time?

- When . . .
  Example: When is happiness a bad emotion?

- Who . . .
  Example: Who decides what art is?

- Can we . . .
  Example: Can we ever know someone else – or even ourselves – completely?

- Why do we say . . .
  Example: Why do we say 'seeing is believing'?

Or my favourite . . .

- What is the difference between . . .
  Example: What is the difference between being a friend and being friendly?

All these question stems are productive. The last one is my favourite because of the sheer range of possibilities it offers us. English has so many words and therefore so many synonyms, which give rise to a huge array of possibilities for comparison and definition.

Below I have listed some examples of comparisons between synonyms and/or antonyms.

What is the difference between . . .

- . . . love and hate?
- . . . stories and lies?

- . . . thinking and believing?
- . . . names and nicknames?
- . . . happiness and contentment?
- . . . the five senses and the Sixth Sense?
- . . . sport and war?
- . . . watching and dreaming?
- . . . reality and virtual reality?
- . . . trying and achieving?
- . . . art and entrepreneurship?
- . . . children and adults?
- . . . wisdom and experience?
- . . . knowledge and evidence?
- . . . fame and infamy?
- . . . rights and responsibilities?
- . . . collaboration and individuality?
- . . . inspiration and dedication?
- . . . good and bad?
- . . . democracy and dictatorship?
- . . . faith and trust?
- . . . power and aggression?

5 Choose the best question

To begin with, it is enough to encourage your children to pick their 'favourite' question. If you are working with a group, this can be done in any number of ways, such as:

Single vote

Each person gets one vote. The question that attracts the most votes is chosen for further discussion.

Omni-vote

Each person can vote as many times as they like (although it is worth reminding younger children that if they all vote for all the questions, there won't be one that stands out!) The omni-vote is generally the best method of voting for groups new to P4C.

Multi-vote

Each person gets a set number of votes – say, three – which can then be spread between three questions or placed onto one or two questions.

Single transferable vote

This works well if you lay out the questions on the floor and ask each child to stand next to one of the questions. You can then ask the children standing next to the questions with fewest votes to recast their vote onto one of the front-runners.

Whether you are choosing questions as a group or with an individual child, it is a good idea to help them learn how to pick the 'best' question. To do this, they will need to create some criteria.

These might be questions that:

- offer the widest selection of possible answers;
- deal with concepts most central to their lives;
- raise the most contestable concepts;
- provide the greatest chance of differing viewpoints;
- can't be answered with a simple yes or no.

It may not be obvious which is the 'best' question and in some regards it may be impossible to decide for sure. However, the very process of selecting criteria and using these to make a decision can be a worthwhile end in itself.

6 First words

This stage is all about encouraging children to share their first responses to the chosen question.

If you are with a group of children, give everyone some reflection time and before inviting first thoughts from a few volunteers. Resist the temptation to question or challenge too soon – and encourage all the other children to listen attentively and with respect.

Do *not* feel compelled to get every child to speak!

There is a commonly held belief that we should try to ensure all children say at least one thing in each discussion. I think this is nonsensical because there are some people who do their very best thinking when saying *nothing* (while others find it easier to think well by talking lots).

One way to justify what I'm saying can be found in the work of Katharine Cook Briggs and her daughter, Isabel Briggs Myers. During World War II, they created the Myers-Briggs Type Indicator (MBTI) to help women identify the sort of wartime jobs in which they would be most comfortable and effective. Their work was based on the theories of Carl Jung.

Of the four pairs of preferences proposed in the MBTI assessment tool, one pair focussed on the difference between 'extroversion' and 'introversion'. It identified that some people tend to 'act–reflect–act' (extroversion), whereas others 'reflect–act–reflect' (introversion). Or, put another way:

Introverted thinking is about: *thinking to talk*

Extroverted thinking is about: *talking to think*

Of course, this is a personality test and should therefore be taken with a pinch of salt. It is also context-related: how many of us are introverted when dragged to a party of complete strangers, but then extroverted when playing host at our own party?

The key is that some people – children included – find it easier to think if they don't have to say anything whereas others find talking lots helps clarify their thinking. Contrast this with many school-based discussions in which the teacher begins by saying: 'I'm going to pass this 'fluffy owl' around the circle. When you've got it then, and only then, is it your turn to talk!'

Imagine if you're in the mood for some introverted thinking and you're given the fluffy owl first. What do you do? Everyone is looking at you expectantly but you haven't had time to think what you might say. As the pressure builds, the teacher reminds you to say pass if you want to. The problem is you know if you *do* say pass, then everyone will think you're a dimwit. Meanwhile, around the other side of the circle, there's an extroverted thinker desperate to say something, with words and ideas ready to pour out of every orifice! Eventually, the extroverted child shouts out and the teacher barks at them for breaking the rules. Oh, the joys of teaching (and yes, so very many times, I *was that* teacher).

Better ways to run discussions that encourage thinking in both an extraverted *and* introverted manner include the following:

Reflection time

Giving everyone a moment to either collect their own thoughts, or to share their first ideas (very quietly) with the person next to them.

Pause

Pausing the P4C session as soon as the favourite (or, preferably, the best) question has been chosen. Then reconvening after everyone has had time to think – either overnight or subconsciously during another activity.

Inner-circle and outer-circle

This works particularly well if you have a group of twenty or more. Split the group in two. Half the children sit in an inner circle, the others sit outside. The outer group can then record the dialogue – with a mind map, concept map or similar – as well jot down their own thoughts. If you then swap the groups around periodically – perhaps every 10 minutes or so – then everyone will have a chance to reflecting quietly *and* speak if they want to.

I realise many teachers will still worry if some children don't speak. However, we don't know that children are concentrating even if they *do* speak! Many children have learned phrases and tactics designed to give the impression that they are focussed when actually their mind is elsewhere. Being honest, how many married couples have also learned the same thing?!

So whether you are in discussion with one child or a whole class of youngsters, I would recommend the following:

(a) *Pause and reflect time.*

(b) *Feasibility language*: Phrases such as 'perhaps', 'maybe', or 'I was wondering' promote a sense of open-mindedness and exploration – which is something that's vital for inquiry.

(c) *Thinking*: Remind children that the most important thing is to *think* about the question. So long as everyone does that, it is up to individuals whether or not to share their views with others.

7 Build and challenge

Once children have shared their first thoughts, begin building on, and/or challenging, the ideas expressed.

Ways to build

RPC (Repeat–Paraphrase–Connect)

When a child has expressed their first idea, we can get others to *Repeat* word for word what they've said; or *Paraphrase* by saying the same thing in a different way; or *Connect* what was said to an idea of their own.

Meaning

A particularly effective strategy is to respond to a child's contribution by asking if anybody else knows what the child meant. Some children will feel certain they understood – so ask them to explain. If there's just two of you in the discussion then you could try explaining what you think the other person meant. Either way, make sure you then ask the first person if indeed that was what they meant. Usually, the explanation is close to the intended meaning but not exactly so, which gives the first person an opportunity to clarify their thoughts even more. This strategy also teaches us there is often a marked difference between what someone says and how others understand it.

Agree

A simple (and effective) convention is to ask everyone taking part in a discussion to begin their first few responses with: 'I agree with . . . because . . .' as this requires participants to listen carefully to what has been said before.

Questions that build

There are many questions that invite children to express themselves further and to build on what has already been said. Examples of these include:

- Can we think of an example of that?
- What are the strengths of that idea?
- Why do you say that?
- Are there any other reasons you can think of?
- What evidence is there to support what you are saying?

Ways to challenge

Disagree

As with the 'I agree' convention, this is a simple and effective approach that aids thinking. This time everyone should begin their responses with 'I disagree with . . . because . . .'.

Create Cognitive Conflict

As I explained on p. 74, setting up a conflict of opinions within an individual's mind causes that person to reflect more urgently on what it is they actually think. This in turn leads to greater engagement and a more energetic search for a resolution. One of the easiest ways to set up cognitive conflict is to use:

If A = B then does B = A?

For instance, if I ask what a holiday (A) is and a child responds: 'not being at school' (this is B), I can then ask: does this mean that if I'm not at school, then I'm on holiday? For example – every evening and weekend? Or if I'm too ill to go to school?

For more examples of this approach, see pp. 74–9.

Critical thinking

The word 'critical' comes from the Greek, *kriticos*, meaning 'able to make judgements'.[47] I find this to be a useful reminder when running P4C sessions: are my children expressing received ideas or are they weighing up pros and cons and making a reasoned judgement?

If it is the latter then they are probably engaging in critical thinking. If it is the former then, no matter how articulate they might be, they may still only be engaging in opinionated debate.

Below are some steps for developing critical thinking. There are many more of course, including the application of formal and informal logic, as well as judgement-making, but the following are good starting points.

(a) Ask for reasons to support the opinions already expressed. For example, if a child has said: 'I think it is wrong to lie', then ask them to give a reason (e.g. because then people won't trust you).

(b) Develop a critical thinking 'argument'. This is a claim that is intended to be persuasive, has a conclusion and is supported by at least one reason.

(c) Examine the quality of each claim in terms of credibility, assumptions they might be based upon, response to counterclaims and so on.

Questions that challenge – there are many questions that invite children to examine what they, and others, have said. These include:

- What alternative ways of looking at this are there?
- How can we verify or disprove that assumption?
- What would happen if the opposite were true?
- What are the weaknesses of that idea?
- What are the consequences of that assumption?

So now you must choose . . . Are you a child who has not yet become world-weary? Or are you a philosopher who will vow never to become so? To children, the world and everything in it is new, something that gives rise to astonishment. It is not like that for adults. Most adults accept the world as a matter of course. This is precisely where philosophers are a notable exception. A philosopher never gets quite used to the world. To him or her, the world continues to seem a bit unreasonable -bewildering, even enigmatic. Philosophers and small children thus have an important faculty in common. The only thing we require to be good philosophers is the faculty of wonder.

(*Sophie's World* by Jostein Gaarder)[48]

---

8 Search for truth

A common definition of philosophy is that it is 'the search for truth'.

We might not necessarily be able to *find* the truth (examples of questions we might never know the truth about include: Are ghosts real? and Why are we here?) However, philosophy is not so much about finding the answer but about the *process* of seeking it. As Einstein said: 'The search for truth is more precious than its possession.' Similarly, the German mathematician Carl Friedrich Gauss (1777–1855) wrote: 'It is not knowledge, but the act of learning, not possession but the act of getting there, that grants the greatest enjoyment.'

So with all the philosophical questions that you encourage children to think about, help them to persevere in their quest for an answer. In one sense, P4C is akin to sailing into a headwind – you need to tack from side to side – while always striving to make progress towards your destination.

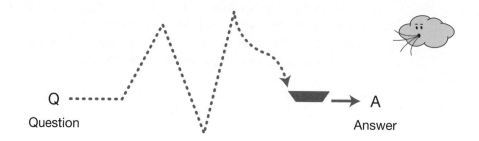

FIGURE 7.2 Moving from question to answer with P4C

One thing to listen out for is the complaint that everyone has a different opinion and therefore the quest for truth is futile. This usually means 'stop asking me difficult questions!'

A practical response to this complaint would be to acknowledge the variety of personal opinions but point out that searching for what these views might share in common enables us to communicate effectively with others. This can be highlighted by showing a Venn diagram in which each circle represents one person's view and the shaded sections represent the areas of commonality between everyone's views.

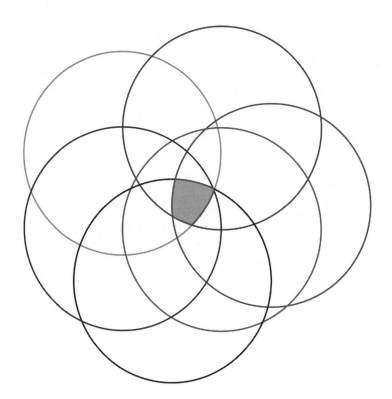

FIGURE 7.3 Common characteristics are represented by the centre point

9 Construct an answer

Even if a question is patently open-ended and philosophical with no agreed answer, children can still feel frustrated if they do not arrive at *an* answer. In school, and often at home, we tend to lead children to believe that learning is about finding the right answer to every question. Yet there are many questions that do not have one, agreed right answer. For example: 'What is the best work-life balance?'; 'What can we do about climate change?'; 'What is the right thing to say to someone who is grieving?'; 'Why do seemingly good people commit atrocities?'

To help children steadily learn that many questions do not have one 'right' answer, I would advocate leaving at least some philosophical questions unanswered, even after a long and fruitful inquiry. This will also help children learn how to manage uncertainty.

That said, it might be more constructive, particularly in the early stages of your children's philosophical development, to help them come to *some* sort of resolution. It is likely that the process of inquiry will have generated a myriad of possibilities. To help children sort through these, you could help them to make links using one of the following approaches.

Ranking

Choosing the best of the bunch. For example, if they have been thinking about friendship, your children will probably have considered such qualities as trust, familiarity, enjoying each other's company, wanting to spend time with each other, knowing the bad as well as the good about each other, a shared history, and so on. So you could now ask them to rank these qualities from most important to least important, or most common to least common. Alternatively, you could ask them to select the *three* qualities that they believe are necessary for *every* friendship.

Relationships

Describing the underlying concept of the question *in relation to another concept* often helps children to shape their ideas more satisfactorily. For example, identifying what a friend is in relation to a best friend; what courage is in relation to foolhardiness; what reality is in relation to make believe, and so on.

Categorise

Using tools such as Venn diagrams (see p. 69 for an example) or Inference squares (see p. 64) can help children distinguish between two (or more) inter-related concepts.

Use a Venn diagram to draw distinctions between help and advice or between telling lies and being wrong. Use an Inference square to separate what we know for certain from what we think we know or would like to know. These strategies can bring clarity to children's (and adult's) thinking.

10 Final words

It is often a good idea to give children a sense of closure by opting for one of these approaches.

Last words

Give every child a final opportunity to respond to the question or to something they have heard during the inquiry. If you have been thinking together with a large group, it might be appropriate to offer the opportunity only to those who haven't spoken, or to allow some children to pass.

Voting

Round off the question by taking a vote. Ensure there are three options: 'yes', 'no' and 'not sure'. Including the 'not sure' option emphasises that most philosophical questions are not black or white but tend to be 'shades of grey'.

Final five

Restrict the number of words each participant can use in the final words to five. Not only does this prevent some children waffling on for ages but it also tends to focus the minds of everyone involved, encouraging them to select only the most pertinent or significant words.

Questions

A phrase that I think captures the spirit of inquiry nicely is: 'Not all of our questions answered, but all of our answers questioned.' So asking all participants to verbalise the questions they still have about the topic would capture the inquiring spirit nicely.

Putting P4C into practice

Enough with the theory! Here are a couple of sequences for you to try with children. The first begins with *The Gruffalo*, so is suitable for children between the ages of four and twelve. The second uses a video made by a student from Larvik in Norway and is suitable for teenagers. There are *lots* more examples on my website, www.challenginglearning.com

The Gruffalo by Julia Donaldson and Axel Scheffler

1 Sit in a circle

If there are more than just two or three of you, make every effort to sit in a circle. This will support the reflective, collaborative nature of inquiry.

2 Read or watch *The Gruffalo*

The book is widely available. Video versions can be found on YouTube, including an all-action one involving some eight-year-olds and me. The animated version by the BBC seems to be aired every Christmas.

3 Draw out the main concepts

Begin by asking children what they think the main ideas of the story were, or what Julia Donaldson was trying to teach young children by writing the story. The concepts my children focussed on included:

- telling lies
- believing others
- existence (of the *Gruffalo*)
- being brave
- being scared
- feeling stupid (when the animals realised they'd been lied to by the mouse)
- talking animals
- survival of the fittest
- cunning.

4 Create philosophical questions

Here are examples of some of the question stems put together with a selection of the concepts. Ideally, your children will do this themselves but this should give you some inspiration.

- What is bravery?
- What makes someone believable?
- Would you be stupid if you believed someone who was telling a lie?
- How do we know that animals can't talk the way humans can?
- Is it always good to be brave?
- What if animals could talk to us?
- Is it possible to be cunning and stupid at the same time?
- Can telling lies ever be a good thing?
- What is the difference between being brave and being stupid?
- Can we be sure there's no such thing as a *gruffalo*?

5 Choose the best question

For example: 'Can we ever be sure there's no such thing as a *gruffalo*?'

6 First words

For example, 'I've never seen a *gruffalo* so I know they're not real'; 'there might be creatures very similar to *gruffalos* that live in undiscovered forests somewhere'; 'I'd love *gruffalos* to be real'.

7 Build and challenge

Questions that would help to build children's ideas include

- Can we think of an example of something we've never seen but we know exists?
- Why do you say that you'd love *gruffalos* to be real?
- Are there any other reasons you can think of to suggest that *gruffalos* are real but just haven't been discovered yet?
- What evidence is there to support your idea that there might be creatures very similar to *gruffalos* alive on the planet?
- Could anyone say why he or she agrees with what 'A' thinks?

Questions that might challenge children's ideas

- Do we have to see something to believe it?
- If I've never seen a duck-billed-platypus, does that mean they aren't real?
- What are the consequences of assuming that if we think we've seen something then that makes it real?
- What would happen if the opposite were true – that *gruffalos* were real but scientists kept them (and other creatures) hidden from us?
- How can we verify or disprove the assumption that anything is real?

8 Search for truth

A classic story to talk about when thinking about existence and reality is Plato's story of the cave.

This is about a group of prisoners chained up at the bottom of a cave, who spend their whole lives staring at the wall in front of them. Eventually one of the prisoners is released. As his eyes adjust to the light outside the cave, he sees the real world in front of him. This amazes him because until then he'd only ever seen the shadows bouncing around the walls of the cave. Feeling sorry for the prisoners he left behind, he returns excitedly to tell them all about the real world he has seen outside the cave. However, since his eyes are no longer used to the darkness of the cave, he stumbles and falls causing his fellow inmates to suspect he has turned blind. When he describes the world outside, the other prisoners refuse to believe him, thinking him mad and so ostracise him. The other prisoners never do get to witness the real world outside.

Plato's story prompts the question: are we like the prisoners in the cave, witnessing only the shadows of the real world? And how can we be sure either way? Though it might be a stretch to then talk about *gruffalos*, how do we know that *gruffalos* don't exist? Perhaps Julia Donaldson is the prisoner that was released and this is her way of telling us about the real world?

9 Construct an answer

An inference square would be a suitable strategy to help children make more sense of their thinking at this point.

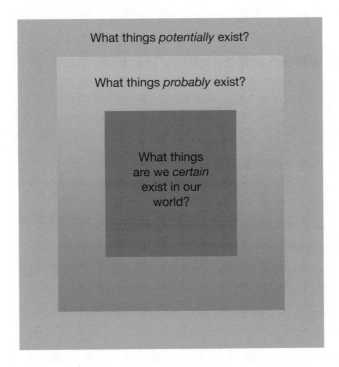

FIGURE 7.4 An inference square

10 Final words

I'd be inclined to go either for a vote, or for identifying any further questions we could ask.

Vote: Can we ever be sure that there's no such thing as a *gruffalo*?

Options: Yes; No; Not sure.

You could then go for a follow-up question, asking children whether their opinion has changed during the discussion and, if so, why.

Further questions about the question

- How could we know whether the world we're in is the real one or not?
- Can we trust our five senses or is it best to rely on our sixth sense instead?
- Which are you most likely to trust – something you see, something you hear, or something you touch?
- Is there a difference between knowing and believing?
- Which creature that we know about is most like a *gruffalo*?
- If *gruffalos* exist, which creatures do you think they live with?
- If you met a real-life *gruffalo*, what would you do?

Jeg Går En Tur – A self-portrait by Lasse Gjertsen

Jeg Går En Tur is a 3-minute video made by a student in Larvik, Norway. The commentary (with English subtitles) and themes are amusing and thought-provoking and the animation work is superb. You can find it on *YouTube* by searching for 'Lasse Gjertsen' or by going to my *YouTube* channel, jabulani4. Teenagers, particularly, will love it.

1 Sit in a circle

2 Watch the video

It's probably worth watching it once for enjoyment and then a second time to record the concepts.

3 Concepts

In one sense, there are almost too many concepts – which is why I recommend you watch the video a second time (perhaps pausing it now and then) to capture as many as possible. The main concepts identified by a group of 14-year-olds I worked with recently include:

- Identity (or being 'me')
- Names
- Indifference ('whatever')
- Change
- The future
- I think, therefore I am
- Beliefs
- Everything is possible

- Understanding each other
- Heaven and hell.

4 Create philosophical questions

Here are some of the questions my group of 14-year-olds created:

- How can I be sure who I really am?
- Why is indifference frowned upon?
- Would you be the same person if you had a different name?
- Are we really able to change the future or do we just like to think we can?
- Is it right to say 'I think, therefore I am', or should it be 'I am, therefore I think'?
- What if no one could understand each other?
- What if everyone in the world *had* to speak the same language?
- Is everything possible in animation?
- Are we responsible for our own beliefs or do they come from our parents and from society?
- Who says whether change is positive or negative?
- Why do we say there is a heaven and hell?

5 Choose the best question

For example: 'Are we responsible for our own beliefs or do they come from our parents and from society?'

6 First words

For example: 'When I was little, I believed what my parents told me. Now I don't'; 'We're definitely influenced by others but I think we then make up our own minds'; 'No one tells us what to think.'

7 Build and challenge

Questions that would help build participants' ideas include

- Can you think of an example of beliefs that have been (a) passed on by your parents, (b) passed on by society, or (c) created on your own?
- What makes beliefs so important?
- Are there any reasons you can think of to support the claim that we're definitely influenced by others?
- Why do you say that you are in charge of your own beliefs?
- What evidence is there to support the idea that we decide our own beliefs?

Questions that might challenge people's initial ideas include:

- What alternative ways of developing beliefs are there?

- How can we verify or disprove that our beliefs are our own?

- What would happen if all beliefs (or no beliefs) came from society?

- What are the weaknesses of the idea that we're in charge of our own beliefs?

- What are the consequences of believing something that nobody else does?

8 Search for truth

Philosophers generally use the term 'belief' to refer to the attitude we have whenever we regard something to be true.

In everyday language, we typically use the word belief to mean something akin to 'values' – belief in God, equality, freedom of speech, and so on. Yet, in philosophy, beliefs also refer to rather more mundane things – belief that I am sat on a chair, that there is an empty coffee mug in front of me, and so on. Furthermore, contemporary philosophers argue that we hold many beliefs despite never having reflected actively on some of them.[49]

These are important distinctions to make: first, we do not need to have reflected systematically on something to hold a belief about it; and second, belief is much the same as an attitude – in other words, our actions reveal our beliefs. This should prove fertile ground for inquiry with teenagers: if I act in a racist or sexist way, does that mean I hold racist or sexist beliefs? If I hold many beliefs that I've never thought about – such as the belief that the sun will rise tomorrow, that I am me and not someone else, or that we should queue for things – then where did they come from? Could I really say they are my own beliefs, or are they the beliefs of others given to me (or programmed into me)?

Another possible avenue to explore is 'predictably irrational behaviour' – a topic explored by behavioural economist Dan Ariely in a video on TED.com (search for 'Are we in control of our own decisions?').

At 02.26 minutes on the video, Ariely presents an optical illusion similar to the one shown in Figure 7.5.

Ariely explains that even though we can prove to ourselves that the two black lines are exactly the same length, we will still 'view' them as very different. In other words, we are being predictably irrational – we *know* they are the same and yet we persist in viewing them as different.

This could be a useful metaphor when talking with teenagers about knowing that all races (or both sexes) are equal, yet continuing to treat each other differently, or knowing what appropriate behaviour is and yet continuing to behave inappropriately.

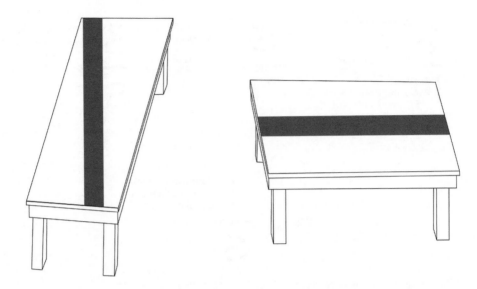

FIGURE 7.5 Ariely's optical illusion (see p. 124)

9 Construct an answer

A Venn diagram could be a productive way to sort out the different types of beliefs we hold. For example, complete or edit the following:

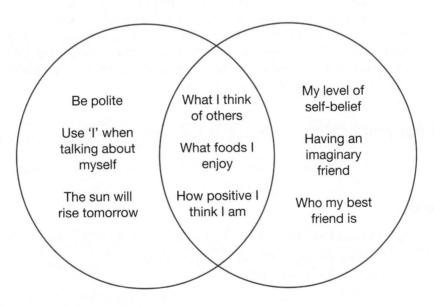

FIGURE 7.6 Venn diagram

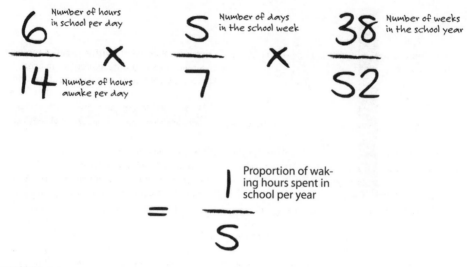

FIGURE 7.7 Calculation showing the proportion of waking hours in a school in a year

10 Final words

The matter of belief is so obviously a philosophical question that very few people will feel the need or the ability to finish with a definitive agreed answer.

That said, it might be worth trying to think of examples of beliefs we hold that have not been influenced in any way, shape or form by other people. I really struggled with the Venn diagram on the previous page because I couldn't think what would definitely go in the corresponding section, 'Beliefs created by me.' If you or the teenagers you are thinking with come up with any possibilities, please post them on the website: www.challenginglearning.com.

Further reading

There are many excellent resources for P4C. Here are a few of my favourites.

Books

P4C Pocketbook by Barry Hymer and Roger Sutcliffe (ISBN: 978–906610418)

The Complete Philosophy Files by Stephen Law and Daniel Postgate (ISBN: 978–1444003345)

Thinking Together by Philip Cam (ISBN: 978–0868065083)

Why Think? Philosophical Play from 3–11 by Sara Stanley (ISBN: 978–1441193605)

Websites

www.p4c.com – International P4C Cooperative

www.sapere.org.uk – UK based charity supporting P4C

www.fapsa.org.au – Australian P4C association

www.p4c.org.nz – P4C in New Zealand

www.icpic.org – International council for P4C

Notes

> The secret to creativity is knowing how to hide your sources.
>
> (Einstein, 1875–1955)

1   From 'The man who invented management: Why Peter Drucker's ideas still matter', *Business Week*, 28 November 2008

2   Binet, A., *Les Idées Modernes sur les Enfants*, Paris: Flammarion, 1909, p. 47

3   Mischel, W., Ebbesen, E. B. and Raskoff Zeiss, A., *Journal of Personality and Social Psychology*, 21(2), 204–18, February 1972

4   Nietzsche, F., *Writings from the Late Notebooks*, Cambridge: Cambridge University Press, 2003, p. 188

5   Peale, N. V., *Positive Thinking Every Day: An Inspiration for Each Day of the Year*, New York: Touchstone, 1993, p. 132

6   Wigfield, A. L. and Eccles, J. S., 'Expectancy-value theory of achievement motivation', *Contemporary Educational Psychology*, 25, 68–81, 2000

7   Hattie, J., *Visible Learning: A synthesis of over 800 meta-analyses relating to achievement*, Oxford: Routledge, 2009, p. 47

8   From the International Football Hall of Fame. www.ifhof.com/hof/charlton.asp (accessed 26 February 2013)

9   From the Guardian newspaper on 25 July 2011. www.guardian.co.uk/education/2011/jul/25/secondary-school-streaming?cat=education&type=article (accessed 26 February 2013)

10 From the Guardian newspaper on 11 May 2009. www.guardian.co.uk/education/2009/may/11/education-policy-class-bias (accessed 26 February 2013)

11 Hart, B. and Risley, T. R., *Meaningful Differences in the Everyday Experience of Young American Children*, Baltimore, MD: P. H. Brookes, 1995

12 Binet, A., 1909, op. cit. p. 95

13   Binet, A., 1909, op. cit. p. 22

14   Binet, A., 1909, op. cit. p. 96

15   Terman, L. M., *The Measurement of Intelligence*, Cambridge, MA: The Riverside Press, 1916, pp. 91–2

16   Hattie, J., 2009, op. cit. p. 47

17   Marzano, R. J., Pickering, D. J. and Pollock, J. E., *Classroom Instruction that Works: Research-based Strategies for Increasing Student Achievement*, Alexandria, VA: ASCD Publications, 2001, p. 88

18   Marzano *et al.*, 2001, op. cit. p. 86

19   Dweck, C. S., *Self-theories: Their Role in Motivation, Personality and Development*, Oxford: Taylor & Francis, 2000, p. 2

20   Mueller, C. M. and Dweck, C. S., 'Implicit theories of intelligence: Malleability beliefs, definitions, and judgements of intelligence', *Journal of Personality and Social Psychology*, 75(1), 33–52, 1998. Copyright 1998 by the American Psychological Association, Inc: 0022-3514/98/S3.00

21   Mueller, C. M. and Dweck, C. S., 1998, op. cit. p. 42

22   From http://mindshift.kqed.org/2012/01/girls-and-math-busting-thestereotype (accessed 26 February 2013)

23   See www.barryhymer.co.uk (accessed 26 February 2013)

24   This figure is unpublished but was mentioned by Prof. Dweck at each conference I co-hosted with Prof. Hymer in June 2010 (see www.caroldweck.co.uk)

25   Dweck, C. S. *Mindset: The new psychology of success*. New York: Random House, 2006, p. 39.

26   Butler, R., 'Task-involving and ego-involving properties of evaluation: Effects of different psychology feedback conditions on motivational perceptions, interest, and performance', *Journal of Educational Psychology*, 79(4), 474–82, 1997

27   For details about the conferences I hosted involving Prof. Dweck, visit www.carol-dweck.co.uk (accessed 26 February 2013)

28   Einstein, A., *Out of My Later Years*, London: Thames & Hudson, 1950, p. 36

29   Dolya, G., *Vygotsky in Action in the Early Years*, Oxford: Routledge, 2007, p. 9

30   From GCSE History B (Modern World) Paper 1 (Core Content with The USA, 1919–1941) published by OCR and sat by pupils on Tuesday, 3 June 2008. Photograph is copyright of Corbis (www.corbis.com)

31   Nottingham, J. A., *Challenging Learning*, first published 2010 by JN Publishing, Berwick-upon-Tweed, UK.

32   See www.edwdebono.com/debono/po.htm (accessed 26 February 2013)

33   Burningham, J., *Would You Rather*, London: Red Fox, 1994

34   Dweck, C. S., 2006, op. cit., p. 4

35   James, W., *The Principles of Psychology*, ed. Miller, G. A., Cambridge, MA: Harvard University Press, 1983, p. 85

36   Nottingham, J. A., 2010, op. cit. p.165

37   Quoted in Nottingham, J. A., 2010, op. cit. p.185

38   From Creating a More Equal and Productive Britain – A lecture by Professor James Heckman on www.youngfoundation.org/events/a-lecture-professorjames-Heckman (accessed 26 February 2013)

39   Newell, A., *Unified Theories of Cognition*, Cambridge, MA: Harvard University Press, 1994

40   Branden, N., *Six Pillars of Self-esteem*, London: Random House, 2004

41   Ginott, H. G., *Between Parent and Child* (2nd edn), New York: Crown Publications, 2004

42   Lipman, M., *Thinking in Education* (1st edn), Cambridge: Cambridge University Press, 1991, p. 42

43   See http://en.wikipedia.org/wiki/Curiosity_killed_the_cat and www.phrases. org.uk/meanings/curiosity-killed-the-cat.html (accessed 26 February 2013)

44   Fry, S., *The Fry Chronicles*, Kindle edn, September 2010, location 1265-6

45   See www.p4c.com for an explanation of the aims, history and principles of Philosophy for Children

46   Humphrys, J., Today, BBC Radio 4, broadcast 26 August 2004

47   Full entry, from etymonline.com 1583, from L. critics, from Gk. kriticos 'able to make judgments', from kinetin 'to separate, decide'. The English word always had overtones of 'censurer, faultfinder'. Critical in this sense is from 1590; meaning 'of the nature of a crisis' is 1649

48   Gaarder, J., *Sophie's World*, Kindle edn, July 2010, location 47

49   From www.seop.leeds.ac.uk/entries/belief/#4 (accessed 26 February 2013)